SPORTS in
AMERICA
1970–1979

TIMOTHY J. SEEBERG
AND JIM GIGLIOTTI

SERIES FOREWORD BY LARRY KEITH

☑®

Facts On File, Inc.

1970–1979
Sports in America

Facts On File, Inc.
132 West 31st Street
New York NY 10001

Library of Congress Cataloging-in-Publication Data

Sports in America / produced by the Shoreline Publishing Group.
    v. cm.
Includes bibliographical references and indexes.
Contents: [1] 1910-1919 / by James Buckley, Jr. and John Walters — [2] 1920-1939 / by John Walters — [3] 1940-1949 / by Phil Barber — [4] 1950-1959 / by Jim Gigliotti — [5] 1960-1969 / by David Fischer — [6] 1970-1979 / by Timothy J. Seeberg and Jim Gigliotti — [7] 1980-1989 / by Michael Teitelbaum — [8] 1990-2003 / by Bob Woods.

ISBN 0-8160-5233-6 (hc : set : alk. paper) — ISBN 0-8160-5234-4 (hc : v. 1 : alk. paper) — ISBN 0-8160-5235-2 (hc : v. 2 : alk. paper) — ISBN 0-8160-5236-0 (hc : v. 3 : alk. paper) — ISBN 0-8160-5237-9 (hc : v. 4 : alk. paper) — ISBN 0-8160-5238-7 (hc : v. 5 : alk. paper) — ISBN 0-8160-5239-5 (hc : v. 6 : alk. paper) — ISBN 0-8160-5240-9 (hc : v. 7 :alk. paper) — ISBN 0-8160-5241-7 (hc : v. 8 : alk. paper)

1. Sports—United States—History.   I. Buckley, James, 1963-   . II. Shoreline Publishing Group. III. Facts on File, Inc.

GV583.S6826 2004
796'.0973'0904—dc22

2004004276

Facts On File books are available at special discounts when purchased in bulk quantities for businesses, associations, institutions, or sales promotions. Please call our Special Sales Department in New York at (212) 967-8800 or (800) 322-8755.

You can find Facts On File on the World Wide Web at http://www.factsonfile.com

Produced by the Shoreline Publishing Group LLC
President/Editorial Director: James Buckley Jr.
Contributing Editors: Jim Gigliotti, Beth Adelman
Text design by Thomas Carling, Carling Design, Inc.
Cover design by Pehrsson Design and Cathy Rincon
Index by Nanette Cardon, IRIS

Photo credits: Page 1: Courtesy Sports Immortals, Inc. These three signed jerseys were worn by members of the Pittsburgh Steelers, who won four Super Bowl (NFL) championships in the 1970s. The players represented are (from top) "Mean" Joe Greene, Terry Bradshaw, and Jack Ham. Read more about Pittsburgh's great NFL teams on pages 49, 50, 59, and 82. All interior photos courtesy AP/Wide World except for the following: Corbis: 3, 27, 46, 48, 59, 81. Sports icons by Bob Eckstein.

Printed in the United States of America.

VH PKG 10 9 8 7 6 5 4 3 2 1

This book is printed on acid-free paper.

CONTENTS

Tennis star Jimmy Connors (page 46)

FOREWORD

BY LARRY KEITH

IN THE FALL OF 1984, STUDENTS AT COLUMBIA University's prestigious Graduate School of Journalism requested that a new course be added to the curriculum—sports journalism.

Sports journalism? In the graduate program of an Ivy League institution? Get serious.

But the students were serious, and, as students will do, they persisted. Eventually, the school formed a committee to interview candidates for the position of "adjunct professor." As it happened, though, the committee wasn't just looking for a professional sports journalist to teach the course part time. That august body wanted to hear clear and convincing arguments that the course should be offered at all.

In other words, did sports matter? And, more to the point, should an institution that administered the Pulitzer Prize, the highest award in journalism, associate itself with the coverage of "fun and games?"

Two decades later, I am pleased to say that Columbia did decide to offer the course and that it remains in the curriculum. With modest pride, I confess that I helped make the arguments that swayed the committee and became the new adjunct professor.

I reflected on that experience when the *Sports in America* editors invited me to write the Foreword to this important series. I said then, and I say now, "Sport is an integral part of American society and requires the attention of a competent and vigilant press." For our purposes here, I might also add, "because it offers insights to our history and culture."

Sports in America is much more than a compilation of names, dates, and facts. Each volume chronicles accomplishments, advances, and expansions of the possible. Not just in the physical ability to run faster, jump higher, or hit a ball farther, but in the cognitive ability to create goals and analyze how to achieve them. In this way, sports, the sweaty offspring of recreation and competition, resemble any other field of endeavor. I certainly wouldn't equate the race for a gold medal with the race to the moon, but the essentials are the same: the application of talent, determination, research, practice, and hard work to a meaningful objective.

Sports matter because they represent the best and worst of us. They give us flesh-and-blood examples of courage and skill. They often embody a heroic human interest story, about overcoming poverty, injustice, injury, or disease. The phrase, "Sports is a microcosm of life," could also be, "Life is a microcosm of sports." Consider racial issues, for example. When Jackie Robinson of the Brooklyn Dodgers broke through Major League Baseball's color barrier in 1947, the significance extended beyond the national pastime. Precisely because baseball *was* the national pastime, this important event reverberated throughout American society.

To be sure, black stars from individual sports had preceded him (notably Joe Louis in boxing and Jesse Owens in track and field), and others would follow (Arthur Ashe in tennis and Tiger Woods in golf), but Robinson stood out as an important member of a *team*. He wasn't just playing with the Dodgers, he was traveling with them, dressing with them, eating with them, living with them. The benefits of integration, the recognition of its humanity, could be appreciated far beyond the borough of Brooklyn.

Sports have always been a laboratory for social issues. Robinson integrated big-league box scores eight years before the U.S. Supreme Court ordered the integration of public schools. Women's official debut in the Olympic Games, though limited to swimming, came in 1912, seven years before they got the right to vote. So even if these sports were late in opening their doors, in another way they were ahead of their time. And if it was necessary to break down some of those doors—Title IX support since 1972 for female college athletics comes to mind—so be it.

Another area of social importance, particularly as it affects young people, is substance abuse. High school, college, and professional teams are united in their opposition to the illegal use of drugs, tobacco, and alcohol. In most venues, testing is mandatory and tolerance is zero. Perhaps the most celebrated case occurred at the 1988 Olympic Games, when Canada's Ben Johnson surrendered his 100-meter gold medal after failing a drug test. Some athletes have lost their careers, and even their lives, to substance abuse. Other athletes have used their fame and success to caution young people about submitting to peer pressure and making poor choices.

Fans care about sports and sports personalities because they provide entertainment and identity. But they aren't the only ones who root, root, root for the home team. Government bodies come on board because sports spur local economies. When a city council votes to help underwrite the cost of a stadium or give financial advantages to the owners of a team, it affects the pocketbook of every taxpayer, not to mention the local ecosystem. When high schools and colleges allocate significant resources to athletics, administrators believe they are serving the greater good, but at what cost? These decisions are relevant far beyond the sports page.

In World War II, America's sporting passion inspired President Franklin Roosevelt to say professional games should not be cancelled. He felt the benefits to the national psyche outweighed the security risk of gathering huge crowds at central locations. In 2001, another generation of fans also continued to attend large-scale sports events because to do otherwise would "let the terrorists win." Being there, yelling your lungs out, cheering victory and bemoaning defeat, is a cleansing, even therapeutic exercise. The security check at the gate is just another price of stepping inside.

Unfortunately, there's a downside to all this. The notion that "Sports build character" is better expressed "Sports *reveal* character." We've witnessed too many coaches and athletes break the rules of fair play and good conduct, on and off the field. We've even seen violence and cheating in youth sports, often by parents of a (supposed) future superstar. We've watched fans "celebrate" championships with destructive behavior. I would argue, however, that these flaws are the exception, not the rule, that the good of sports outweighs the bad, that many of life's success stories took root on an athletic field.

Any serious examination of sports leads, inevitably, to the question of athletes as role models. Pro basketball star Charles Barkley created quite a stir in 1993 when he declared in a Nike shoe commercial, "I am not paid to be a role model." The knee-jerk response was, "But kids look up to you!" Barkley was right to raise the issue, though. He was saying that, in making lifestyle choices in language, clothing, and behavior, young people should look elsewhere for role models—ideally in their own home, to responsible parents.

The fact remains, however, that athletes occupy an exalted place in our society, at least when they are magnified in the mass media, and especially in the big-business, money-motivated sports. The athletes we venerate can be as young as a high school basketball player or as old as a Hall of Famer. (They can even be dead, as Babe Ruth's commercial longevity attests.) They are honored and coddled in a way few mortals are. We are quick—too quick—to excuse their excesses and ignore their indulgences. They influence the way we live (the food on our table, the cars in our driveway) and think (Ted Williams inspired patriotism as a fighter pilot during World War II and the Korean conflict; Muhammad Ali's opposition to the Vietnam War on religious grounds, validated by the Supreme Court, inspired the peace movement). No wonder we elect them—track stars, football coaches, baseball pitchers—to represent us in government. Meanwhile, television networks pay exorbitant sums to sports leagues so their teams can pay fortunes for players' services.

It has always been this way. If we, as a nation, love sports, then we, quite naturally, will love the men and women who play them best. In return, they give us entertainment, release, and inspiration. From the beginning of the 20th century until now, *Sports in America* is their story—and ours.

Larry Keith is a former writer and editor at Sports Illustrated. *He covered baseball and college basketball and edited the official Olympic programs in 1996, 2000 and 2002. He is a former adjunct professor of sports journalism at Columbia University and is a member of the Board of Visitors of the University of North Carolina School of Journalism.*

INTRODUCTION
1970–1979

A subject that had been a huge and constant part of sports in America since the late 1800s rose to new and pervasive prominence in the 1970s: Money. And a subject that had NOT been a big part of sports in America began to play a much larger part on the athletic scene: Women. Those two themes defined nearly all of the major events and issues of the decade.

First, money: Buoyed by an influx of money from ever-growing rights fees paid by network television, pro sports franchises were suddenly very lucrative enterprises. The athletes who made those leagues and teams go found themselves, in many cases, receiving a disproportionately small part of that new-found wealth. They turned, like so many Americans, to the courts for help. In baseball, the Curt Flood case in 1969 had been the first salvo in a war between players and owners that continues to this day. But it was in the 1970s that the players made their first and largest steps, beginning with the death of the "reserve clause" that bound a player to a team for life and continuing with the creation of free agency following the Andy Messersmith case (see page 57). Now baseball became a bidding war between teams, with superstar players being offered larger and larger contracts. Similar deals were being struck in football as its own reserve system was dismantled by court cases. Basketball and hockey's salary wars were some years off, but the writing was on the wall. Success in sports would now be measured not so much in wins or losses but by paychecks.

Another part of the growing influence of money on sports was the rise of rivals to the established pro leagues. Businesspeople shut out of the existing leagues saw an opportunity to satiate the public's thirst for sports by starting their own leagues. The American Basketball Association had started in 1968, but had its heyday in the 1970s. The World Football League tried to challenge the NFL in 1974, but failed two years later. The World Hockey Association gave Wayne Gretzky his first pro job, but by the end of the decade, the National Hockey League had swallowed up the best of the upstart league. The common fate of all these leagues was their disappearance, but they gave athletes a way to leverage their services and force teams to compete on salary. While the men's pro sports world was spending as much time in courts as on them, a hugely important sports event

Equal Rights *Women all over the country demanded gender equality in the 1970s—on and off the playing fields.*

happened in the halls of Congress in 1972. As part of the large Education Amendments Act, Congress included a section known as Title IX, which essentially forced schools to provide equal access to sports for women. Prior to the Act, college sports participation by women was a fraction of that by male athletes. In the years and decades afterward, female participation (and the attention their exploits received from the media and fans) skyrocketed. Women's pro sports, spurred by the success of Title IX and the ongoing movement for increased women's rights in all aspects of society, also experienced a boom.

Though the events of the Munich Olympics in 1972 (page 29) were not directly related to American sports, the tragedy there brought the sports world into a clash with the "real" world in what was the most public and tragic way.

While most remembered for that tragedy and the epochal changes in finances and gender balance, the 1970s also saw many memorable performances. And though sometimes dismissed as a polyester decade with bad fashion and too-long hair, events from the 1970s continue to have resonance in today's sports world. Every time a player signs another $100 million contract, he can look to the athletes of the 1970s and say thanks. And every time another girl enjoys the benefits of athletics, she can point to the pioneering work done by female athletes in the 1970s.

1970

Pro Football Becomes One Happy Family

In 1970, four years after a monumental agreement to merge, the 10-member American Football League (AFL) officially joined the National Football League (NFL). The merger formed a 26-team NFL made up of two conferences, each with three divisions.

The NFL style of play had been defense-oriented and was dominated by running plays on offense. Almost all the NFL teams used the same formations and the same tactics. The AFL featured a flashier and more diverse style. The ultimate contest between these two styles of play was Super Bowl III on January 12, 1969. The Baltimore Colts of the NFL were favored by anywhere from 18 to 22 points, but the game proved to be the most colossal upset in Super Bowl history. The New York Jets beat the Colts by a score of 16–7.

Like all great upsets, Super Bowl III created myths that linger to this day. The greatest of these was that the game somehow brought about the NFL-AFL merger. In fact, simply by agreeing in 1966 to match their champions in a Super Bowl, the two leagues were agreeing to a merger; what came about in 1970, when the two leagues realigned, was a mere formality. No one wanted a continuation of the bidding war that had driven the salary of an untested New York Jets rookie named Joe Namath to an unheard-of sum of $450,000. And Namath was far from the only bonus baby of his era. In fact, the year after Namath was drafted in 1965, the old-guard Green Bay Packers forked over an astounding $1 million for rookie running backs Donnie Anderson and Jim Grabowski.

The eight original AFL owners, who were nicknamed "The Foolish Club," gave football fans a game with wide-open, exciting offenses and high scores. The NFL, meanwhile, was known for its vicious defenses and conservative offenses. Clear-cut wins by the Jets and the Kansas City Chiefs (also of the AFL) in Super Bowls III and IV, respectively, evened the tab at two wins apiece between the two leagues. By the time of the 1970 merger, the AFL was clearly as good as the NFL. In fact, former AFL teams won five of the first seven post-merger Super Bowls, which might even suggest that the NFL had somehow absorbed the better league.

Tennis Royalty *Billie Jean King leveraged her stature as the queen of women's tennis to help spawn a new tour for women (see page 12).*

A Challenge Leads to Baseball's Biggest Change

 At the age of 31, star outfielder Curt Flood (b.1938) sacrificed his career in Major League Baseball to make a point. His action—a lawsuit against Major League Baseball—is considered by many to be the pioneering act in baseball labor relations.

Lost and Won *Outfielder Curt Flood (shown here with the Washington Senators in 1971) lost his day in court but helped foster changes in baseball's long-standing reserve clause.*

After a short stint as an infielder with the Cincinnati Reds, Flood was traded to the St. Louis Cardinals in 1958 at the age of 18. The Cardinals moved him to centerfield, where he played for the next 12 seasons. Flood's hitting ability and defensive skills made him one of the best all-around players in the National League. In 1964, Flood batted .311 with 211 hits to tie for the lead in the National League. In 1963, he won the first of seven consecutive Gold Gloves. In 1967, he made an error in the outfield to end record streaks of 568 consecutive chances and 227 games without an error. In 1964, 1966, and 1968 Flood represented the Cardinals in the annual All-Star Game.

It was off the field, however, that Flood carved a cornerstone position in baseball's history. Following the 1969 season, the Cardinals set up a trade with the Philadelphia Phillies. St. Louis sent Flood, Tim McCarver, Joe Hoerner, and Bryon Browne to the Phillies for Richie Allen, Cookie Rojas, and Jerry Johnson.

Flood didn't want to play in Philadelphia and decided in 1970 to file a lawsuit against Major League Baseball over the reserve clause. Baseball's reserve clause, a standard part of baseball contracts since the founding of the National League in 1876, said that a player belonged to the team that held his contract. Flood wanted the freedom to choose who he would play for, even though he was making $90,000 (a princely sum at the time). He compared "being owned" in baseball to "being a slave 100 years ago."

The lawsuit was a gamble for Flood. He was just 31 years old and in the prime of his career. Still, he decided the risk was worthwhile. His challenge of the reserve clause was based on the idea that it violated antitrust legislation, which says all the business owners in an industry can't band together to control the industry. The U.S. Congress had created a special exemption from this antitrust legislation for Major League Baseball.

Flood's case was heard before a Federal Court in New York. He lost his $4.1 million antitrust lawsuit, but federal judge Irving Ben Cooper recommended in his judgement that changes be made in baseball's reserve system, to be achieved through negotiations between players and owners. Within six years, the judge's recommendations forever changed the face of baseball's labor negotiations.

Flood and his lawyers appealed the case to the U.S. Supreme Court and Flood decided to sit out the 1970 season. Meanwhile, the Washington Senators made a deal with the Phillies for Flood's "reserve." After determining that accepting the assignment would not hurt his case, Flood agreed to play for the Senators in 1971. Early in the 1971 season, Flood felt he had become the target of ill will in baseball. In response, he left the Senators and moved to Denmark; meanwhile, his lawsuit continued.

On June 18, 1972, the U.S. Supreme Court upheld the lower court's ruling against Flood. This decision by the country's highest court enabled baseball to

King Is Queen of Women's Tennis

In 1962, Billie Jean King won her first Wimbledon title, defeating the world's number-one player, Margaret Smith-Court. Four years later, King captured her second Wimbledon championship and the ranking of number one player in the world. Returning to her hotel with her silver trophy, she found on her bed the closest thing to prize money that big-time tennis paid in those days: six candy bars left by some of her friends. Tennis was, until 1968, almost exclusively an amateur sport. The enormous rewards and celebrity associated with women's tennis today are available, in very large part, thanks to Billie Jean King.

Clearly a dedicated and proven player, King perhaps achieved her most significant accomplishments off the court. An ardent spokeswoman for women's tennis, she fought to get people to take the women's game seriously. Without hesitation or concern for any possible negative ramifications, she encouraged her fellow pros (both women and men) to demand fair pay. She spoke out against tournament committees and promoters who treated women as second-class citizens, sometimes paying the women as little as 10 percent of the prize money they paid the men.

Much of what King did for women's tennis, she did behind the scenes, earning her neither money nor publicity. Ironically, it was for a 1973 event she considered silly that she received a good deal of both. For her defeat of a former Wimbledon men's champion, Bobby Riggs (1918–1995), in the much-hyped "Battle of the Sexes" challenge match (see page 40), she received a check that almost equaled her total winnings from that monumental 1971 season. And, silly or not, that match captured the attention of a record tennis crowd (30,472) and a national television audience.

In 1974 she became the first woman—in any sport—to coach a professional team containing men when she served as player-coach of the Philadelphia Freedom of World Team Tennis, a short-lived pro tennis league she and her husband, Larry King, helped establish.

King won 67 pro and 37 amateur singles titles, and reached 38 other pro finals with a 677–149 singles match record as a professional. In 1990, at the age of 46, playing in a cameo role in a tournament in Florida in 1990, she won a doubles match with her 13-year-old pro rookie partner, Jennifer Capriati.

1970

continue to be exempt from antitrust laws and maintain its reserve clause. The decision, however, was very narrow and left the door open for legislation or collective bargaining to undermine the reserve clause. By the end of the year, the Major League owners brought an end to the reserve clause by agreeing to salary arbitration, in which an impartial arbitrator would work with teams and players on contested contracts.

Flood never played again in professional baseball. His impact on the game, however, continues today, reflected in the enormous salaries paid to top players in the sport.

Women's Professional Tennis Serves an Ace

Angry about the treatment of women in professional tennis and realizing the women had to separate from the men to achieve recognition and significant prize money on their own, tennis stars Billie Jean King (b.1943) and Rosie Casals (b.1948) went on a public relations campaign. They started by talking to Gladys Heldman, the publisher of *World*

Tennis magazine. Then King worked tirelessly to promote the idea to fellow players, the public, and the media, and to secure corporate sponsorship for a women's-only tour. Her efforts resulted in tobacco giant Phillip Morris' financial support for and Heldman's management of the Virginia Slims Championship.

That inaugural tournament, held on September 23 and 24, paved the way for the next year's launch of a complete Virginia Slims circuit, which included 14 tournaments and quickly became an extremely profitable and popular tour. By the end of the decade, the total annual prize money on the Virginia Slims Tour jumped from $250,000 to more than $6 million.

The Best Offense Is a Great Defenseman

In 1970 Bobby Orr (b.1948) of the Boston Bruins radically redefined the role of a National Hockey League (NHL) defenseman. As the first "offensive" blueliner (a nickname for a defenseman, who normally plays behind the blue line on the ice that denotes a team's defensive zone), he set the single-season assists record with 87, led the league in scoring with 33 goals, and was named MVP. His famous "flying goal"—scored as he leaped horizontally above the ice—clinched the Bruins' Stanley Cup sweep of the St. Louis Blues in overtime of game four in April.

Orr, arguably hockey's greatest defenseman ever, changed the way hockey is played with his revolutionary approach to his position. The 6-foot-one, 200-pound Bruin struck fear into the hearts of opposing players and coaches with his

To Students of Bobby Orr . . .

"To students of Bobby Orr, the spectacular has become routine, and the routine has become unacceptable. One of a defenseman's primary jobs is to get the puck out of his own end and down the ice, and some players carry out this task with all the grace and ease of a starving man eating a pomegranate through a screen door. Orr does it routinely."

—Jack Olsen, *Sports Illustrated*, December 21, 1970

A Sports TV Pioneer

When he died in 2002, Roone Arledge was praised as the greatest innovator in the history of sports television. His supporters had a good argument. From *Wide World of Sports*, which he created in 1961, to 1970's debut of *Monday Night Football*, to his ground-breaking productions of Olympic Games, Arledge changed the way the world watched sports.

In *Wide World of Sports* and ABC's NCAA (National Collegiate Athletic Association) football in the 1960s, Arledge introduced slow-motion and freeze-frame views, instant replays, hand-held cameras, and the placement of microphones that brought the sounds of the game into living rooms.

In addition to all the technical innovations, Arledge will also be remembered for putting the focus on the person involved in the sport—getting up close and personal with the athletes. Arledge, who had been named president of ABC Sports in 1968, supervised coverage of 10 Olympics from 1964 to 1988, including the memorable 1972 Games in Munich, Germany, which were disrupted by a terrorist attack (see page 29). Arledge expanded Olympics broadcasts beyond the competition by including personal profiles of athletes, a style echoed today by his protege, Dick Ebersol, who runs NBC Sports, a regular broadcaster of Summer and Winter Olympics.

superior vision and uncanny knack for finding the puck in wide open ice. In the 1966–67 season, Orr scored 13 goals and 41 total points, which earned him the Calder Trophy as the NHL's outstanding rookie. Beginning with the 1969–70 season, Orr posted point totals of 120, 139, 117, 101, 122, and 135 for the next six seasons, an awesome feat at the time for any player, but particularly remarkable for a defenseman.

Orr led the "Big Bad Bruins" to two Stanley Cup championships, in 1970 and 1972. After his tenure with the Bruins ended, Orr signed with the Chicago Blackhawks in June 1976. However, a series of knee injuries limited his playing time in his final three seasons and he retired in 1978 at the age of 30.

Orr's legacy of "offensive defenseman" continues today, and nearly every NHL team boasts all-around players at every position.

Turning Sweat into Show Business

Few people expected the September 21 debut of ABC's *Monday Night Football* to mark the beginning of the most successful prime-time program in television history. Probably even fewer anticipated the show would have such a lasting impact on the way television presents sporting events to the public. Three people, however, did believe they could use *Monday Night Football* to change Americans' relationship with sports.

When Pete Rozelle (1926–1996) accepted the job of NFL commissioner in 1960, one of his first accomplishments was also his most visionary. The 33-year-old Rozelle recognized immediately that, more than a business composed of football teams, the NFL was an unparalleled marketing machine. As the NFL's exposure on television grew, so did its popularity.

Other Milestones of 1970

✔ Perhaps the most important innovation in tennis scoring, the tiebreaker was invented by Jimmy Van Alen and instituted at the 1970 U.S. Open. Previously, sets could last hours, because players had to win by at least two games to capture the set. The tiebreaker shortened and enlivened matches and soon reformed the scoring system everywhere.

✔ Former AFL star quarterback Jack Kemp was elected to the United States Senate, representing New York. After a highly successful career in which he led his teams to five AFL Championship Games and two league titles, Kemp started on a long career in politics, including stints in Congress and as Secretary of Housing and Urban Development under the first President Bush.

✔ The Pittsburgh Pirates started a fashion trend that eventually swept through all of baseball. Introducing the first radical departure in the design of baseball uniforms, the Pirates wore form-fitting uniforms made of double-knit polyester. Players welcomed the new material because it weighed far less than the traditional wool uniforms, was cooler, and allowed better freedom of movement.

✔ On September 13, 55 runners finished the first New York City Marathon, which was produced with a total budget of $1,000. From this humble beginning, the race has grown to become a weeklong, worldwide celebration. The event now includes 30,000 athletes, 12,000 volunteers, thousands of city employees, more than 2 million spectators lining the course, and tens of millions more television viewers around the globe.

✔ Gary Gabelich, driving a rocket-powered car, set the world land speed record of 622.407 miles per hour on October 23.

Larry Mahan

✔ On November 8, New Orleans Saints placekicker Tom Dempsey not only beat the Detroit Lions with the game-winning field goal, but put himself in the NFL's record books. His 63-yard field goal surpassed the previous record by a full seven yards and remained unmatched until 1998. Amazingly, Dempsey was born without a right hand and with no toes on this kicking foot.

✔Margaret Smith-Court became the second woman to win the Grand Slam of tennis, capturing the U.S., French, and Australian Opens, and Wimbledon in the same year. In her career, Smith-Court won 24 Grand Slam singles titles, part of a record 62 total Grand Slam titles.

✔ Larry Mahan became the first rodeo cowboy to win five consecutive titles as All-Around Cowboy Champion at the National Finals Rodeo in December. Mahan won a sixth All-Around title in 1973.

But when this trend reached a plateau in the late 1960s, Rozelle decided the league needed to find a way to reach a broader audience. His idea was to play a game each week on Monday nights, putting prime time football into the living rooms of every American.

NBC and CBS both declined Rozelle's offer to televise Monday night games, because they could not imagine that housewives and advertisers would ever prefer football to traditional prime-time programming. However, Roone Arledge (1931–2002; see the box on page 13), the revolutionary president of ABC Sports, had a vision that complemented Rozelle's. Arledge's network was a distant third in the ratings and needed to make a bold move. *Monday Night Football* was that bold move.

Monday Night Football was not about football as America had come to know it. Arledge recognized that sports events are always dramas, with a beginning, middle, and end, and he also understood why these dramas were not as appealing to a mass audience as he thought they could be: There was no narrator carrying the plot. There was no depth to the characters. There was no "middle man" helping the audience connect with the players on the field. Arledge took care of all those shortcomings with one move. He invited Howard Cosell (1920–1995) to the announcers' booth and let him change sports television forever.

Cosell was a lawyer and a broadcaster with a grating, nasal voice, and a melodramatic style. His opinions were unlike those of any other sportscaster, and he challenged the audience to think about more than just the action on the field. Almost overnight, what he said and did during *Monday Night Football* re-energized sports television. Tuesday morning conversations among fans were as much about Cosell's opinions as about the game itself. He became the most-loved and most-hated voice in sports.

Over the next three decades, *Monday Night Football* was among the most-watched television programs every year. Sports had been brought into America's prime time, and it would never leave.

Never Too Old

The long, gray, thinning hair, the deeply lined face—George Blanda (b.1927) looked old. But he never got old. He just got better. Over 26 incredible professional seasons, he posted a record 2,002 points and an impressive 236 touchdown passes as a kicker and quarterback. But the real legacy of George Blanda is the magic he created as an American folk hero who continued to deliver clutch performances in his fourth decade playing football, until the age of 48.

Blanda was a scoring machine for 10 years as a Chicago Bears kicker, an icy competitor when he finally got his first call as a long-term starting quarterback and led the Houston Oilers to championships in the AFL's first two seasons, 1960 and 1961.

But nothing could match the dramatic impact Blanda brought to the Oakland Raiders from 1967 until his 1975 retirement. In a magical 1970 season, at age 43, Blanda came off the bench in five straight games to deliver a dramatic kick or a touchdown pass that produced a win or a tie.

Blanda was a popular, sometimes testy, leader who played in a record 340 games. He was the epitome of the grizzled veteran, the symbol of everlasting youth. He retired as the NFL's all-time leading scorer with 2,002 points (since surpassed) and was elected to the Pro Football Hall of Fame in 1981.

1971

The Return of "The Greatest"

Three years after his boxing license and World Boxing Championship (WBC) heavyweight title had been stripped following his refusal, based on his Islamic beliefs, to be drafted into the army, Muhammad Ali (b.1942) got both his boxing license and his WBC title back. On June 29, the U.S. Supreme Court overturned his 1967 conviction for evading the draft. However, while Ali had been prohibited from fighting, the World Boxing Association (WBA) had given its heavyweight title to Joe Frazier (b.1944).

Never before had two active fighters simultaneously had a legitimate claim to the same title. Ali's return to the ring for a decisive bout against Frazier would leave only one champion. Appropriately, their titan matchup, billed as "The Fight of the Century," attracted 300 million viewers via satellite and closed-circuit television—more viewers than any boxing match in history.

On March 8 at New York's Madison Square Garden, the smaller Frazier wore down Ali with relentless left hooks, even knocking Ali down for only the third time

in Ali's career. Frazier retained—and became the sole owner of—the heavyweight title.

But Ali was far from finished. Over the next three years, he won 12 of 13 fights, half by knockout. In 1974, Ali got his chance for a long-awaited rematch with Frazier. Although no longer the heavyweight champ, Frazier was still one of the world's best fighters. Ali proved to be better, winning the fight by a unanimous decision.

Later that same year, Ali regained the heavyweight crown, using his "rope-a-dope" strategy to let George Foreman tire himself out by throwing countless punches against Ali's body, but none that did damage. By the eighth round, Foreman was clearly exhausted. Ali threw a knockout punch to win the fight, and he became only the second man in boxing history to regain the world heavyweight championship.

In 1975, Ali defended his title three times. But the bout that will always be remembered from that year was "The Thrilla in Manila," the third and final fight between Ali and Frazier, and still considered one of the greatest fights ever. After 14 grueling see-saw rounds, Frazier's

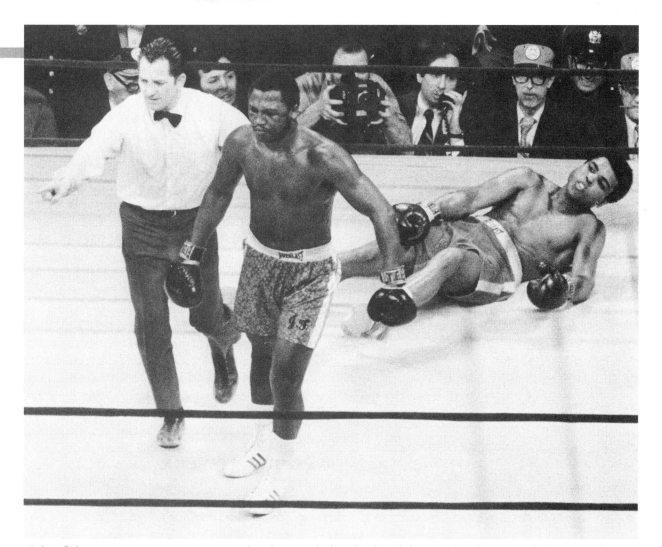

Fight of the Century   *Joe Frazier stunned Muhammad Ali with a knockdown in their heavyweight bout March 8.*

trainer called off the fight, seeing that his man was unable to go another round. Immediately after this, his final and perhaps most spectacular victory, Ali said it was the "closest thing to dying I know of."

New Rival League Makes NHL Stronger

 The World Hockey Association (WHA) was formed in April 1971.

After initially being dismissed by the NHL, the new league quickly proved to be the first legitimate rival to the NHL in 55 years. But ultimately, this competition—for the attention of hockey fans, the talents of the world's best hockey players, and the dollars of corporate advertisers and sponsors—resulted in the NHL becoming bigger, stronger, and more American.

In November 1971, the WHA announced it had 12 teams, eight in the

1971

Hockey's Growth Extends Beyond the Ice

In 1971, the Mississauga (Wisconsin) Ball Hockey Association was founded. Reflecting the increasing worldwide passion for hockey, this league was the first organized street hockey (or roller hockey) league in the United States. The first plastic orange ball, used instead of a traditional black rubber puck, was introduced by Arnold Herka, of Viceroy Rubber, the same year. The street version of this exciting sport has never looked back.

United States and four in Canada. Unlike the NHL, the WHA allowed its teams to sign junior league players younger than 18. The most notable result of that decision was the beginning of the career of the greatest hockey player ever. At 17, Wayne Gretzky (b. 1954) took the ice as one of the WHA's Indianapolis Racers.

The WHA also led the way in scouting and recruiting European players. This changed the professional game, introducing a new style and strategy that placed more emphasis on speed, stickhandling, and passing, and less on brute force.

The new league also went after established NHL stars. The WHA's Winnipeg Jets signed the NHL's legendary Bobby Hull to a million-dollar contract. Other teams offered contracts sometimes three or four times larger than NHL salaries.

To combat the WHA threat, the NHL added two teams: the Atlanta Flames to offset the WHA's presence the South, and the New York Islanders to regain the NHL's prominence in that big-market region. The NHL also settled a WHA-led antitrust lawsuit out of court, agreeing with the WHA to honor one another's player contracts and paying the WHA a settlement fee of almost $2 million. In effect, the WHA had defeated the reserve clause in professional hockey, which had bound players for life to NHL teams.

After growing to as many as 14 teams in 1974–75, the WHA was back down to 12 by 1976. After the 1978–79 season, only six teams remained. At this point, the WHA merged with the NHL, which had grown significantly stronger because of the changes it had made in response to the WHA. Four WHA teams—the Edmonton Oilers, New England (later Hartford) Whalers, Quebec Nordiques (now the Colorado Avalanche), and Winnipeg Jets—survived the merger intact. The other clubs' players were free to sign with NHL teams.

Ping-Pong Diplomacy

In April of 1971, the American table tennis (ping-pong) team traveled to Nagoya, Japan, to compete for the World Table Tennis Championship. The result had little to do with table tennis but much to do with international relations.

While in Nagoya, the American team received an unexpected invitation from their Chinese colleagues. For the first time since the Communists took control of China in 1949, a group of Americans were invited to the People's Republic. The invitation was accepted, and four days later history—not sports history, but diplomatic history—was made.

No one from outside the People's Republic of China could have been prepared for what awaited them at the airport in Beijing. After more than two decades of mutual hostility, Chinese Premier Zhou En-Lai personally greeted the surprised American delegation of "ping-pong diplomats." As the Chinese Premier later said, "Never before in history—and possibly never since—has a sport been used so effectively as a tool for international diplomacy."

It was a savvy gesture. Without making commitments, or even suggestions of any kind, China's gesture promised an easing of tensions in Asia and the possibility of improved trade relations between the two countries. In fact, this move also opened the door for talks with the Soviet Union on crucial matters such as arms control. And only hours after the Premier welcomed the table tennis players, President Richard Nixon announced other initiatives for trade and travel between the

Political Ping-Pong Ball *A table-tennis match helped thaw frigid relations between the United States and communist China.*

1971

United States and the People's Republic of China.

The American table tennis players, led by team captain Jack Howard, faced off against their Chinese opponents at Qinghua University. The Chinese won the men's games 5–3 and the women's game's 5–4. Afterward, the teams exchanged gifts and walked off together hand-in-hand.

Soon after the U.S. team's trip, Secretary of State Henry Kissinger went to Beijing to arrange a presidential visit to China. Seven months later, in February of 1972, President Nixon's journey became one of the most important events in the United States since World War II. One year later, the Chinese team visited the United States.

A Tale of Two Deities

In 1971, when Bobby Knight took the job as head coach of the Indiana University men's basketball team, he was only 30 years old, but he was more than ready for the intense spotlight that would very quickly be pointed in his direction.

The team Knight inherited had come to be known as the "Hurryin' Hoosiers," a team that for years had fit perfectly in the Big Ten—a conference that was popular for its fast, high-scoring style of basketball. Rather than adapt his strategy and style to fit what crowds and players had come to love, Knight instituted the game-slowing, score-reducing man-to-man defense that had been so successful for him as coach at West Point.

It did not take long for the Hoosier fans—and even opposing coaches—to warm up to Knight's more deliberate style of play. In fact, within 10 years of Knight's arrival at Indiana, the average scores of Big Ten games had shrunk by more than five points per team. More important to Hoosier players and fans was the consistently high level of play Knight demanded—and received—from his teams. In his first 20 years as Indiana's head coach, Knight led his team to 10 conference championships and three NCAA titles. He also amassed more victories more quickly in his career than almost any other coach at any level of the game.

As part of his fame, however, Knight's success is second only to his controversial tactics and behavior. Fear and intimidation were key elements of Knight's coaching style. His methods have been widely acknowledged by former players, assistant coaches, faculty members, and school administrators as dehumanizing. Many of his public indiscretions, such as throwing a chair across the court during a game, assaulting a police officer, and taking his team off the floor because of his lack of respect for the officiating, heightened his players' fear of him. The seemingly endless string of questionable behavior also brought tremendous criticism upon Knight, the university, and even college basketball in general.

Nonetheless, Knight was tolerated, even accepted because of the results he produced, both on and off the court. Knight was just as unforgiving of mistakes or apparent lapses in commitment by officials, assistant coaches, and his players. And he was entirely intolerant of inappropriate support from wealthy or influential boosters. As a result of this and other Knight standards, the Hoosiers during Knight's tenure boasted one of the best records of compliance with NCAA rules in Division I-A basketball.

Knight's relentless demand for perfection is the one common denominator found in the tremendous number of Knight's former coaches and players who have gone on to achieve great personal and professional success, in the improved officiating in the Big Ten, and in the elevation of Indiana to a college basketball champion and perennial powerhouse.

Ultimately, though, Knight's behavior became too much. He lost his job in Indiana in 2000, after his volatile temper resulted in a series of incidents. He wasn't out of work long, though, and he now coaches at Texas Tech University.

The Longest Day

Christmas Day 1971 was "The Longest Day" in NFL history, and saw one of the greatest games ever played. In a double-overtime AFC playoff game, the Miami Dolphins beat the Kansas City Chiefs 27–24 when Garo Yepremian kicked a 37-yard field goal. The kick ended a tense drama after 7 minutes and 40 seconds of the second overtime—82 minutes and 40 seconds of game action in all. It remains the longest game in the history of the NFL.

"After 25 years, people remember that game," Chiefs quarterback Len Dawson said in 2003. "People will talk about us beating the Vikings in Super Bowl IV, or they might talk about Super Bowl I, our

Politics and Sports at the White House

Richard Nixon (1913–1994), the 37th president of the United States, formed an unprecedented relationship between politics and athletics. The president's intense personal interest in sporting events was well known, and went far beyond the traditional presidential ceremonial events, such as throwing out the first pitch of the professional baseball season and calling the wining team's locker room after the Super Bowl.

Nixon did these things, but he also went much further. He repeatedly surprised reporters, athletes, and coaches with his detailed knowledge about sporting events, interjected himself twice into disputes about the mythical national championship in college football (called mythical because there is never an actual playoff to determine the champion), and made a surprise visit to a Washington Redskins' practice to give the football team an inspirational boost after a difficult loss. In many ways he was the ultimate fan.

In August, Nixon gave a speech at a dinner the National Football League held in honor of the new inductees into the Pro Football Hall of Fame. In the speech, he said sports help shape a "a spirit of competition, a spirit of trying to do our very best."

1971

loss to the Packers. But they always remember Christmas Day."

The Dolphins forced the overtime sessions when they tied the game at 24–24 on quarterback Bob Griese's five-yard touchdown pass to tight end Marv Fleming with one minute, 36 seconds left in regulation. Chiefs' running back Ed Podolak returned the ensuing kickoff 78 yards to set up a potential game-winning field-goal attempt by Jan Stenerud, but he missed from 31 yards with 35 seconds to go. Stenerud, normally a reliable kicker who eventually made the Hall of Fame, also missed from 42 yards in overtime when his try was blocked. Yepremian also

Other Milestones of 1971

✔ With a 2,495-game winning streak on the line on January 5, the Harlem Globetrotters, basketball's "clown princes" and most entertaining ambassadors, lost to the New Jersey Reds, 100–99. With their next game, the Globetrotters began a new winning streak, which lasted until 1995 and spanned 8,829 games.

✔ Tyler Palmer recorded the United States' first World Cup victory in alpine skiing in St. Moritz, Switzerland, on January 23.

✔ A young graphic designer, Carolyn Davidson, created the swoosh that became the official logo for Nike and, over the next 10 years, a trademark for a society increasingly focused on health and athletics.

✔ Pitcher Satchel Paige was elected to the Baseball Hall of Fame, becoming the first player elected by the newly established Committee on Negro Baseball Leagues.

✔ On August 10, Harmon Killebrew of the Minnesota Twins joined baseball's 500 home run club. Killebrew homered on his 6,671st at-bat, the fewest since 1929, when Babe Ruth hit his 500th on his 5,801st at-bat.

✔ ABC televised a USA–Cuba volleyball match from Havana in August. This was the first time an American

The Orioles won the World Series.

television network sports department covered a sporting event in Cuba since Fidel Castro came to power in 1959.

✔ On October 13, the Pittsburgh Pirates beat the visiting Baltimore Orioles 4–3 in the first World Series night game. NBC called for the later start, figuring it could get higher television ratings at night than during the day—an argument that easily persuaded Major League Baseball, which had been experiencing declines in ratings and stadium attendance over recent years. Within a few years, the majority of baseball's regular-season and post-season games were played at night.

missed a long try (52 yards) in the first overtime, but won it when he got another chance in the second overtime.

Podolak, his red-and-white Chiefs' uniform caked with mud, blood, sweat, and grass, amassed 350 yards and scored two touchdowns in the game. Podolak's total still ranks as the top mark for combined net yards (the combined total of rushing yards, receiving yards, and return yards) in playoff history, and it ranks third in all games in NFL history.

Miami went on to defeat the defending Super Bowl champion Baltimore Colts 21–0 in the AFC Championship Game in January and begin a run of three straight Super Bowl appearances.

Derby Days

In August 1971, the 37-year-old All-American Soap Box Derby let young girls compete for the first time. In the annual race, children hand-build small, motorless cars and then race them on a downhill course. Gravity provides the only power.

The event had begun almost accidentally when a Dayton, Ohio, newspaperman helped some local kids find a place to race their go-karts in 1933. The next year, the first official competition was held in Dayton. One year later, the derby moved to Akron, Ohio. Over time, the event grew to sponsor races in dozens of cities, with local winners advancing to Akron. At first, only boys were allowed to race, but a flowering women's movement

Go, Speed Racers! *The Great American Soap Box Derby, a tradition since 1933, was open to young women for the first time. Five of the 272 participants in 1971 were girls.*

in the 1960s and 1970s helped break this tradition.

Five of the 272 contestants in 1971 were young women. By the next year more than 10 percent of these finalists were girls, two of whom finished among the top 10. Finally, in 1975, 11-year-old Karen Stead became the first girl to win the All-American Soap Box Derby.

1972

Winter Games Controversy

The biggest controversy in the 48-year history of the Winter Olympic Games erupted just three days before the opening ceremonies were scheduled to begin on February 3 in Sapporo, Japan. The International Olympic Committee's (IOC) president, Avery Brundage (1887–1975), threatened to disqualify 40 alpine skiers for violating the IOC's restrictions against professional athletics. Fortunately, the IOC executive committee reached a compromise. It allowed all other "offenders" to participate, but the IOC excluded Karl Schranz, Austrian World Cup champion and skiing's most commercialized star.

The issue of amateur status also caused controversy in the ice hockey tournament. Canada had previously withdrawn its hockey team from international amateur competition to protest the use of "professional amateurs" by the Soviet Union and other eastern bloc countries. When the International Ice Hockey Federation and the IOC denied Canada's request to include NHL players on their Olympic team, Canada refused to send a team to Sapporo. At the time, players in the Communist countries were supposed to be soldiers or police officers or firemen and amateur athletes, but in reality the government paid their salaries and they did nothing but athletics.

Although eastern bloc countries did dominate the Sapporo tournament (the Soviet team won their third consecutive Olympic gold; the Czechs defeated Poland to win the bronze), the Americans finished second—possibly in a position the absent Canadians would have occupied.

For the first time, the only gold medals won by American athletes at these Games were won by women. Anne Henning and Dianne Holum captured speed skating victories, while Barbara Cochran won the slalom skiing event.

Another Kind of Baseball Strike

In 1972, when team owners tried to reduce their payment to the Major League Baseball players pension fund by $500,000, the players decided to fight back: For the first time in baseball history, the players went on strike.

The Major League Baseball Players Association, the players' labor union had

Union Label   *Baseball players, under the direction of union chief Marvin Miller (second from right), went on strike.*

been around for more than 35 years, but its sole purpose was to collect and administer a meager pension. Concerned about getting a piece of growing television revenues, the players sought to strengthen their union in 1965. They hired Marvin Miller (b.1917), a veteran labor organizer who had fought for the United Steelworkers Union. When Miller came on board and saw what the conditions were, he knew much more was at stake than adding broadcasting money to the pension fund.

For one thing, the minimum salary was $6,000, just $1,000 more than it had

been in 1947. As he began to collect data, the players were surprised at how poorly they were being paid. This education paved the way for the first collective bargaining agreement between owners and players in 1968. It provided some modest improvements, but most importantly, it gave the players some leverage. For nearly 100 years, team owners had a "take it or leave it" relationship with players. The union could (and did) file complaints with the National Labor Relations Board when they were treated unfairly. Players also won the right to have their grievances heard before an independent arbitrator.

Baseball's Labor Wars

The players went on strike for the first time in baseball history in 1972. Briefly, here are key dates in baseball labor issues over the next two decades:

1972: The players walked out for 12 days beginning April 1. They gained the right to salary arbitration.

1973: The owners locked out the players from February 8 to February 25, but the season started on time. The owners eventually increased minimum salaries and pension contributions.

1975: Pitchers Dave McNally and Andy Messersmith refuse to sign contracts, battling the reserve clause again (see page 57). An arbitrator upheld these two players' cases in the offseason prior to 1976 (when a 17-day lockout interrupted spring training), and free agency was born.

1980: The players went on strike the final eight days of spring training, but the season started on time after a new working agreement was in place with free-agent compensation a key issue.

1981: A 50-day strike forced the owners to agree to a plan that let players who were not yet eligible for free agency (an earlier agreement had put that time at six years), still have their salaries decided by an arbitrator.

1985: Another player strike, this time only two days long, forced owners to change the way arbitration was arranged.

1988: An arbitrator ruled that baseball owners had unfairly and illegally "colluded," or secretly worked together, to not offer high-paying contracts to free agents. The players were awarded damages from the owners of more than $102.5 million.

1990: Spring training was delayed more than a month when the owners locked out the players, largely over salary cap and arbitration issues.

1994: A terrible impasse between players and owners forced the owners to lock the players out, ending the 1994 season in August and canceling the World Series for the first time in 92 years. A temporary agreement was reached in April 1995 and that season started a few weeks late. Baseball's current labor deal (as of summer 2003) was signed in 1996.

The owners did not like the union interfering in their business, and they especially bristled at the players standing up to them. Curt Flood filed a lawsuit against baseball commissioner Bowie Kuhn in 1970 (see page 9). Flood argued that the reserve clause, which gave teams the absolute right to renew a player's contract for one year, was illegal and, consequently, he should be allowed to negotiate freely with other teams.

Although Flood lost his case, his effort had energized the other players. The volatile situation led to the strike. It lasted just over a week, from April 6 to April 14, wiping out 86 of the season's first scheduled games. The owners settled by giving the players everything they asked for. More significantly, the players learned that through collective action, they could force the owners to make changes (see the box on this page). Baseball would never be the same.

Title IX Makes Women Winners

The Education Amendments Act of 1972 grew out of the Civil Rights and feminist movements of the 1950s,

1960s, and early 1970s. The act was intended primarily to improve the quality and equality of educational opportunities for all Americans. Almost accidentally, one specific part of it brought about one of the most significant changes in American sports.

American society had always put tremendous pressure on women to choose either marriage or a college education and a career. As a result, female athletes were rare and were considered abnormal. Physical education for girls and women was grudgingly offered, but strenuous exercise was discouraged and considered unsafe and unbecoming for a lady. Women in high school and college had few opportunities to compete in sports, and pro sports for women were limited mostly to golf and, just barely, tennis.

On July 1, when the Education Amendments Act of 1972 went into effect, Title IX of that act said, "No person in the United States shall, on the basis of sex, be excluded from participation in, or denied the benefits of, or be subjected to discrimination under any educational program or activity receiving federal aid."

In other words, women count equally with men. That statement has, too slowly for some and perhaps too rapidly for others, continued to find support throughout society. In the classroom, in the workplace, and in leadership, Title IX continues to effect changes in the opportunities available to women.

Title IX's effect on female participation in athletics at the high school and college levels has gained the most public notice. Figures from the National Federation of State High School Associations show that the 2,746,181 females in sports in 2000–2001 is about nine times the number of female participants pre-Title IX in 1971. According to the Chronicle of Higher Education, there were roughly 30,000 female athletes at the college level in

Opportunities for All *Title IX quickly had an effect on women's college sports. By the end of the decade, athletes such as Old Dominion basketball player Nancy Lieberman (above) were stars.*

1972

1972. By 1991, that number had increased to 92,778; by 2001, it was 150,916.

Title IX's effect has been global—women from all over the world attend college and participate in sports in the United States. From professional leagues in basketball and soccer, to the recent inclusion of women in several formerly exclusively male Olympic sports, such as bobsled, basketball, and pole vault, women are receiving more of the sports spotlight previously reserved for men. The change is obvious on the local level, too, as girls in organized leagues and neighborhood pickup games enjoy soccer, baseball, basketball, football, martial arts, and more.

Even with all the evidence of Title IX's success, athletic department spending, especially at the Division I collegiate level, remains grossly uneven. Some schools have cut men's sports in an effort to slow growing budgets. The National Wrestling Coaches Association filed suit against the Education Department in United States District Court in 2003, alleging that Title IX is not being properly interpreted.

Title IX advocates, however, point to alarming spending on football and men's basketball. Even more vigorously, they say the majority of universities are not close to compliance with Title IX. Men still get considerably more funding in athletics than women, and the elimination of some men's programs has not resulted in a meaningful shift toward equity. According to a comprehensive study by the Chronicle of Higher Education, Division I schools in 2000–2001 spent $934.9 million on women's programs compared to $2.7 billion —almost three times more—on men's programs.

Neither the objective of Title IX nor the broader objectives of the entire Education Amendments Act have yet been met. Title IX is not perfect. But it has been—and will continue to be—a force that shapes athletics and our society.

Title IX: Off the Field

Since Title IX was enacted on June 23, 1972, women have made substantial progress in athletics, education, and employment. The number of female college athletes has nearly tripled since 1972, while the percent of high school athletes who are girls has risen to more than 40 percent from less than 10 percent.

But the act had perhaps farther reaching consequences off the playing fields. In 1972, fewer than 10 percent of medical, law, and other doctoral degrees were awarded to women. In recent years, those numbers have risen more than four-fold. Today more than 40 percent of all of these advanced degrees are earned by female students.

Swimming's Golden Boy

Mark Spitz (b.1950) was one of the world's best and most successful swimmers. His record of seven gold medals and seven world records at the 1972 Summer Olympics in Munich, Germany in September will probably never be beaten.

Spitz's first Olympic experience was in the 1968 Olympics. Leading up to those Summer Games in Mexico City, Spitz had boasted several times that he would win six gold medals—a feat no one in any Olympic sport had ever accomplished. His cocky statements alienated him from his teammates. Those statements also

The Games Must Go On

International terrorism collided for the first time with sports at the Summer Olympic Games in Munich, Germany. On September 5, Arab terrorists infiltrated the Olympic Village, home of the Games' athletes, and kidnapped 11 members of the Israeli Olympic team. A two-day standoff stunned and transfixed the world, as the Olympic Games were put on hold.

Tragically, all 11 athletes, five terrorists, and one policeman were killed during an attempt to rescue them as they boarded a helicopter. Even though numerous competitors and officials strongly called for the remainder of the Olympics to be cancelled, the IOC decided to let the Games continue. This decision was based largely on the wishes of the Israeli government and team, who refused to give in to terrorist pressure. Avery Brundage, IOC president, said he would not allow the peaceful spirit of the Olympic movement to be ruined by "a handful of terrorists."

The Munich tragedy signaled an end to the innocent notion that sports could be separate from the cares and troubles of the wider world. Today, heavy security accompanies every major sporting event, and security provisions are a major consideration when the IOC decides what cities host the Games.

proved to be more than he could live up to in 1968. He returned to the United States with only two gold medals, both of which he won in relay competitions. On his own, he won a silver medal in the 100-meter butterfly event and a bronze in the 100-meter freestyle. In the 200-meter freestyle, he came in last.

Disappointed and humbled, the 18-year-old Spitz entered Indiana University on a swimming scholarship. Again, he made more enemies than friends because of his attitude. More often than not, however, his performances in the pool backed up his words. In his four years at Indiana, he led the men's swimming team to four NCAA national championships. He also won more individual and team events than any swimmer in NCAA history.

Then, at 22, Spitz made Olympic history. At the Munich Games, Spitz won the 100-meter butterfly, the 200-hundred meter butterfly, the 100-meter free-style, the 200-meter free-style, the 400-meter free-style, the 800-meter free-style, and the 400-meter medley relay—all in world record time.

Sadly, Spitz was unable to celebrate his accomplishments among his fellow athletes. In the aftermath of the terrorist attack on the Israeli team (see box), many Jewish athletes—including Spitz—were quickly removed from the Olympic Village. Just a few hours after winning his last race, Spitz was flown back to the United States, where he was greeted like the hero he had become.

Three Controversial Seconds

When the Summer Olympics began, no American basketball team had ever lost in men's Olympic play, dating back to 1936. All of this changed on September 10, in a flurry of confusion and controversy. On that morning, the youngest squad ever to represent the

1972

Big Splash *American swimmer Mark Spitz was the star of the Summer Olympics in Munich, where he won a remarkable seven gold medals.*

United States in Olympic basketball competition stepped onto the floor to face their athletic and political enemy, the Soviet Union, in a final battle for the gold medal. The American team had very little experience. Most members were in college, none had played professionally, and as a team, they had been together for only 12 exhibition games before the Olympics and then for the eight games leading up to this point in the Olympic tournament. (Until recently, professional players were barred from participating in Olympic events, so Dream Teams were still decades away.)

By comparison, the Soviets were significantly bigger and much more experienced. They were brilliantly coached and

came into the Olympics having already played approximately 400 games as a team. The Soviets were hardly the underdog. In fact, they promised to be the stiffest competitions the Americans had ever faced.

From the opening tip-off, the Americans were surprised to find themselves playing against a team that was better than they had imagined. By halftime, the United States was down by five points. With less than 10 minutes remaining in the second half, that deficit had doubled to 10. But the Americans battled back. With 38 seconds left, the young squad had closed to within one point. Then, with three seconds left in the game, Doug Collins of the United States team was fouled as he drove to the basket. Standing up to the incredible pressure, Collins sank both free throws. The Americans were up 50–49. This was their first lead of the entire game.

And then time seemed to stop. In fact, that very short span of time kept repeating itself. After Collins' free throw, the Soviets in-bounded the ball. Immediately, the referees stopped the game with one second remaining. In response to an argument from the Soviet bench, the officials put three seconds back on the clock.

The Soviets in-bounded the ball a second time. Almost immediately, the horn sounded signaling the end of the game and, apparently, an American victory. But again, the teams were ordered back on the floor. The officials indicated the clock had not been properly reset to show three seconds remaining before the Soviets had in-bounded the ball.

Order was restored on the court, the clock was again reset to show three seconds remaining and, for a third time, the Soviets in-bounded the ball. Soviet center Alexander Belov caught the full-court pass and scored the winning lay-up as the clock—this time for good—ran out. The Soviets had won.

Immediately, the controversy exploded. Convinced that it had been wronged, the United States team filed a formal protest with the International Basketball Federation and refused to accept their silver medals. Later that afternoon, a five-member panel ruled in favor of the Soviets. American dominance of amateur basketball had, officially, finally, and controversially ended.

Perfect

The NFL was 52 years old before any team won every game it played in a season. And no team since the 1972 Miami Dolphins has yet been able to equal this amazing feat. That the 1972 Dolphins were a strong team was not a surprise. With essentially the same players and led by the same legendary head coach, Don Shula, the Dolphins had finished the previous season with a 10–3–1 record, which included an appearance in Super Bowl VI (they lost to the Dallas Cowboys).

The 1972 season was Shula's third with the Dolphins. Under his strict

Europeans Discover American Basketball

With the dethroning of the United States as the pre-eminent team in international competition, basketball fans everywhere began to see that top talent was no longer developed only in America. European players began to be scouted and signed to play for National Basketball Association (NBA) teams. As basketball has continued to become a more global game, NBA players have gained exposure in Europe and around the world. And players from around the world have gained fame in the NBA, including Hakeem Olajuwon (Nigeria), Patrick Ewing (Jamaica), Toni Kukoc (Croatia), Arvydas Sabonis (Lithuania), and Yao Ming (China). Similarly, American male and female college players not yet considered ready to compete in the NBA or Women's National Basketball Association (WNBA), along with former NBA players looking for competition after their U.S. careers, join European and Japanese professional teams.

1972

no-nonsense approach, the young and enthusiastic but well-disciplined Dolphins gelled into a cohesive unit. The offense was potent, due in no small part to its five future Hall of Famers: running back Larry Csonka, guard Larry Little, quarterback Bob Griese, center Jim Langer, and wide receiver Paul Warfield. But it was the unparalleled effectiveness of its mostly unknown defensive squad that made this edition of the Miami Dolphins famous to fans across the country—and to all the other teams throughout the league.

At a time when NFL teams and their fans celebrated a forceful defense with nicknames such as the Pittsburgh Steelers' "Steel Curtain," the Minnesota Vikings' "Purple People Eaters," and the Dallas Cowboys' "Doomsday Defense," Miami's "No-Name Defense" made up for its lack of glamour by being the backbone of a great team. Eventually, even the "No-Names" of middle linebacker Nick Buoniconti, and defensive linemen Manny Fernandez and Bill Stanfill became familiar names.

Unsuspecting heroes also surfaced from the Dolphins' bench. In week five, with starting quarterback Bob Griese injured, 38-year-old veteran quarterback Earl Morrall stepped in—and stepped up—with experienced leadership and poise to keep the unbeaten streak alive. Morrall, in fact, directed the Miami offense for the remainder of the regular season and to their 20–14 victory over the

Other Milestones of 1972

✔ After more than two months without a defeat, the Los Angeles Lakers of the NBA lost to the Milwaukee Bucks 120–104 on January 10. At 33 games, the Lakers' consecutive game winning streak shattered the previous record of 20, which had been set by the Bucks the season before.

✔ In the WHA's second season, the Houston Aeros signed 45-year-old Gordie Howe, who had retired from the NHL two years earlier. The Aeros teamed him with his two sons, Mark and Matt Howe. Gordie won the league's MVP award, Mark was named rookie of the year, and the Aeros won the WHA championship.

Gordie Howe (left) and sons

✔ On April 20, the Naismith Memorial Basketball Hall of Fame in Springfield, Massachusetts, inducted Bob Douglas (1882–1979), the first African American to be enshrined. Douglas, who organized, owned, and coached the first African-American professional basketball team (the New York Renaissance) beginning in the early 1920s, is considered to be the father of black professional basketball.

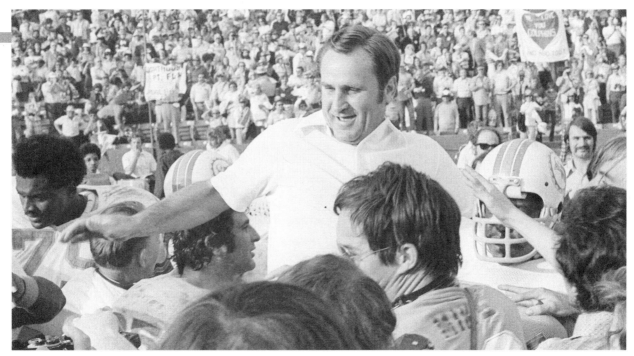

Perfect Finish *Miami coach Don Shula gets a victory ride after his Dolphins finished 17–0.*

Cleveland Browns in the first round of the playoffs.

By week 16 of the season, Griese was back in uniform. In a hard-fought battle against the Pittsburgh Steelers on December 31, it was Griese, this time, who came off the bench to direct his team to a thrilling 21–17 victory and the AFC title.

Two weeks later, on January 14, Griese started and finished Miami's final game of the season, when the Dolphins' miracle season culminated with a 14–7 victory over the Washington Redskins in Super Bowl VII. That made their full-season record to a perfect 17–0, a feat that has remained unmatched.

1973

Westwood Wizardry

By 1972, people had begun referring to the NCAA men's basketball tournament as the "UCLA Invitational," because the University of California at Los Angeles (UCLA) Bruins had won the last five championships and seven of the last eight. The dominance of the 1971–72 team, however, had to be somewhat surprising since the Bruins had lost all but one major player from the year before. Only Henry Bibby, an All-American guard, returned from the 1970–71 team, but he was joined by a number of talented newcomers, including forward Keith Wilkes and center Bill Walton (see the box on page 36). UCLA went 30-0 and averaged 95 points per game, while setting the all-time record for average margin of victory at 30.3 points. Bibby was gone to the NBA by 1973, but with Walton leading the way, UCLA again entered the tournament ranked number one, undefeated, and expected to capture another title.

The team shattered the record for the most consecutive wins—previously held by San Francisco, who won 60 straight games from 1955–57. When the NCAA Tournament started, the Bruins had won 71 consecutive games, dating back to the 1971 season, and had won a record 32 consecutive tournament games. By the end of the 1973 tournament, the Bruins had stretched their winning streak to 75 games, and they captured their seventh consecutive NCAA title.

The championship game in St. Louis, Missouri, on March 26 was the first to be televised in prime time, and a record viewing audience tuned in to watch college basketball's reigning dynasty. UCLA was formidable, but the Memphis State Tigers thought they had a good chance if they could shut down Walton. Memphis State fronted Walton (positioning a defensive player on both sides of an opponent) in an effort to deny him the ball, but the strategy backfired. The Bruins simply lobbed passes above the defense to the 6-foot-11 Walton, who easily converted them into baskets.

Still, Walton spent some of the first half on the bench with three fouls, and the Tigers shot well enough to reach halftime tied at 39–39. But UCLA and Walton exploded in the second half. The big man scored 14 points during a crucial 20–10 run, and the Bruins never looked back. When Walton left the game with a

Alone in Front   *Secretariat breezes to victory in the Kentucky Derby, the first leg of the Triple Crown (see page 38).*

sprained ankle with just under three minutes remaining, the game was no longer in doubt, and he had scored a championship-record 44 points. He also set a record by making 21 of 22 shots.

Knicks Do It Again

While UCLA was dominating college basketball, several teams were competing for the title of best in the pros.

"Big Red" Leads the Blue and Gold

In the second half of the 1973 NCAA championship game against Memphis State University, UCLA head coach John Wooden silently presided over his team's huddle during a timeout. Finally, Bruin guard Greg Lee asked Wooden if the Bruins should try some different plays. Wooden looked at Lee and replied, "Why?" The fact was, the one play the Bruins had relied on all game had been unstoppable: get the ball to junior center Bill Walton.

Walton earned national player of the year honors for the second straight season and was again named the NCAA Tournament's Most Outstanding Player after scoring 44 points, a title-game record. Walton even became the first basketball player since Bill Bradley in 1964 to win the Sullivan Award as the nation's best amateur athlete.

In 1973, the New York Knicks won their second NBA title in four years (they had won in 1970), with one of the most decorated teams in NBA history. The Knicks knocked off the Lakers in the Finals in five games, neatly wrapping up a five-year period in which its main starters were all future Hall of Fame members.

At center, Willis Reed was the heart of the team, a powerful rebounder and inside force who was just as strong a floor leader. Just before the final game of the 1970s Finals, which he was supposed to miss with a severe leg injury, he had famously limped onto the court to the cheers of the Madison Square Garden crowd. Though Reed scored only four points in that game, his "comeback" was the inspiration for the Knicks' first title. In 1973, he helped the defense-oriented Knicks shut down high-scoring Wilt Chamberlain and the Lakers.

Helping Reed on the front line were forwards Dave DeBusschere, a hard-working scorer, and Jerry Lucas, a solid scorer and defender. (Lucas would later go on to a career as a memory coach, teaching people how to use their memories better. While on plane trips with the Knicks, Lucas put his prodigious memory to use by keeping track of the winnings of the various card games going on around him.) In the backcourt, the Knicks boasted a terrific tandem of Earl "The Pearl" Monroe and Walt "Clyde" Frazier. Monroe was an outstanding ballhandler, while Frazier was a sweet shooter known as much for his somewhat outlandish off-the-court wardrobe as his clutch jumper.

Amazingly, all five of these, plus coach Red Holzman, would eventually be inducted into the Basketball Hall of Fame in Springfield, Massachusetts.

Have Bat, Will Travel

For a century, pitchers in baseball were like every other position player—they batted. Then in 1973, the New York Yankees' Ron Blomberg stepped to the plate in the first inning of an Opening Day game on April 6 against the Boston Red Sox' Luis Tiant at Fenway Park. Blomberg went to bat three more times during the game. He never took a position in the field.

Blomberg's at-bat marked the American League's official debut of the designated-hitter (DH) rule, which allowed teams to designate a non-position player to bat instead of the pitcher without affecting the pitcher's status on defense. The debate about the merits of the DH has raged ever since. Purists believe it detracts from the game, while others welcome the extra offense it provides.

The 1973 introduction of the DH was part of a two-year experiment approved by the American League as an attempt to bolster its attendance, which was lagging behind the National League. The new rule increased offense—the Kansas City Royals put the world of baseball on notice on Opening Day when they knocked ace pitcher Nolan Ryan out of the game in just the third inning with the first of three consecutive home runs hit against the California Angels—and did bring more fans to the ballpark.

In 1976, Rule 6.10(b) was made permanent, but it still applies only to baseball's American League. The National League is still virtually the only organized baseball league that does not use the DH in its games. High schools, colleges, minor-league teams, and international baseball associations have all adopted the DH rule.

Over the years, designated hitters have tended to be used primarily to add

Designated Hitter *The Yankees' Ron Blomberg made history when he became the first DH in big-league annals.*

The Ryan Express

Every pitcher's dream is to throw a no-hitter, and approximately 98 percent of them never accomplish that dream. Nolan Ryan managed to do it seven times, and no pitcher in the history of the game has even come close.

In 1973, the first year of the designated hitter (see page 36), Nolan Ryan, pitching for the California Angels, threw the first two of his seven no-hitters. He blanked the Kansas City Royals on May 15 for a 3–0 victory. He then no-hit the Detroit Tigers 6–0 on July 15 while striking out 17 batters. He was only the fourth pitcher to throw two no-hitters in one season.

A fireballing righthander, Ryan struggled with his control throughout his career. But when he was pitching around the plate, he was virtually unhittable. Ryan set a new single-season record in 1973 by striking out 383 batters.

Ryan later played for the Houston Astros and the Texas Rangers and kept winning and striking players out. He ended his remarkable career in 1993 at age 46, with 324 victories, and he is the all-time leader in no-hitters, strikeouts, and walks. He also pitched for more seasons (27) than any other player in the history of the game.

---

power to the lineup. A couple of DHs, however, have added some speed. Paul Molitor of the Milwaukee Brewers became the first DH to steal more than 20 bases in 1987, when he had 23. He broke his own record with 24 in 1992. His record was broken in 1998 when Jose Canseco, the Toronto Blue Jays' DH, stole 29 bases.

Windsurfing Is Big Fun and Big Business

The beginning of windsurfing can be traced to 1965, when two good friends, Hoyle Schweitzer and Jim Drake, wanted to combine surfing and sailing. They realized that the major problem with surfing was that you had to wait for the waves. By the end of 1968, they patented the first windsurf board, called the Windsurfer. In 1973, they licensed their concept to the Ten Cate Company, and for the next five years Windsurfers took American thrillseekers by storm.

The King of the Sport of Kings

When Secretariat won the Kentucky Derby and the Preakness Stakes—the first two legs of the Triple Crown—his performances amazed even those who had predicted greatness for the colt when he was named Horse of the Year as a two-year-old. At the Derby on May 5, he rallied from last place to win in record time. Two weeks later, at the Preakness, Secretariat won again by two and a half lengths, and only a clock malfunction prevented him from breaking another official race record.

Only the Belmont Stakes stood between Secretariat and the first Triple Crown in 25 years. On June 9, 70,000 fans packed Belmont Park in New York as Secretariat and four other horses were led to the gate. Secretariat shared the early lead with Sham, who had finished second in the Derby and the Preakness, but the pace quickened as they neared six furlongs. Secretariat pulled away, and his trainer, Lucien Laurin, worried that the horse could not maintain his speed all the way to the end of the race. His lead, however, continued to increase as Secretariat reached the third turn. He just kept getting faster.

The roar of the crowd welcomed Secretariat as he thundered home. There was no horse within 31 lengths when Secretariat crossed the finish line in a time of two minutes, 24 seconds—almost three full seconds faster that the previous track record and one of the most decisive victories in horse racing history. Secretariat had won not only the first Triple Crown in 25 years, but also the hearts of a nation and a permanent place in horse racing history as one of its greatest champions.

The Juice

In the 1970s, America embraced Buffalo Bills running back O.J. Simpson as it had few other black athletes. Simpson (known as "the Juice" because of his initials) was breaking records on the football field, running through airports for the Hertz rental car company—as the first black celebrity to be featured in a national ad campaign—and deflecting praise to his offensive line. In less than a decade, he'd become the single most popular figure in American team sports—a black hero whom white kids adored. In a mid-70s poll of grade-schoolers, Simpson was voted the nation's most admired figure, by both girls and boys.

On the field, from his first game for the University of Southern California (USC) Trojans in 1967, it was apparent that he not only was taller, stronger, and heavier than most running backs of the period, but he was also faster than virtually all of his peers. In fact, he became the prototype running back of the next generation. In addition to winning the Heisman Trophy in 1968, Simpson led the Trojans to a national title in 1967, thanks to his memorable 64-yard touchdown run to beat cross-town rival UCLA, 21–20.

Selected by the abysmal Buffalo Bills as the first pick of the 1969 NFL draft, he languished for three years in a pass-oriented offense. But Lou Saban arrived in 1972 as the Bills' head coach, and he quickly realized that he should not just be using the game's best running back as a decoy. As a result, Simpson made history. In 1973 he broke Jim Brown's all-time single-season rushing record, finishing with 2,003 yards in 14 games, the first player ever to top 2,000 yards in a season (only four other players have since gone over the 2,000-yard mark). Simpson might have been even better in 1975, when he accounted for 2,243 combined yards (rushing and receiving), scored 23 touchdowns, and led the league's most prolific offense. He did this while running behind an offensive line dubbed the "Electric Company," because they "turned on the Juice."

Simpson, a six-time Pro Bowl selection, retired in 1979 after two seasons with the San Francisco 49ers, with 11,236 rushing yards and 2,142 yards more on 203 career receptions.

Sadly, in 1994 he ended up on the opposite end of the popularity scale. He was tried on charges that he murdered his ex-wife and her friend. The country

1973

became obsessed with the trial, and his acquittal on criminal charges was roundly criticized. He was found liable for the murders in civil court, and remains an unpopular figure.

Butkus Retires; Running Backs Relieved

He was a grunting, snarling, snorting defensive machine, dedicated to creating football mayhem and destroying offensive game plans. Dick Butkus' road to the Pro Football Hall of Fame was paved with blood, sweat, pain—and the intense anger that coursed through the veins of this most celebrated middle linebacker.

The 6-foot-3, 245-pound Butkus served as the Chicago Bears' defensive leader and enforcer from 1965 to 1973, when the almost-constant physical

Other Milestones of 1973

✔ On January 10, his 24th birthday, George Foreman defeated Joe Frazier to win boxing's heavyweight title.

✔ On March 1, Robyn Smith became the first woman jockey to win a stakes race (a race for which an owner pays an entry fee for his or her horse; that fee usually is part of the total prize money for the race) when she rode North Sea to victory at Aqueduct.

✔ The first Iditarod Trail Sled Dog Race was run across the Alaska wilderness beginning on March 3. The approximately 1,150-mile race from Anchorage to Nome usually takes about 10 days to two weeks and tests the skill and endurance of both humans and dogs.

✔ On September 20, Billie Jean King beat former Wimbledon men's champion Bobby Riggs in the "Battle of the Sexes." Her victory was seen by a television

Steve Prefontaine

audience estimated at more than 50 million people worldwide, a huge number at the time.

✔ Steve Prefontaine became the first major track athlete to wear Nike shoes. "Pre," who never lost a race in four years at the University of Oregon, embodied the competitive spirit of the new brand. His success and personality helped convert several athletes to Nikes, including Jon Anderson, who won the Boston Marathon, and Romanian tennis player Ilie Nastase, the top-ranked pro.

✔ Johnny Unitas was the most celebrated football passer in history when he retired in 1973 after one season with the San Diego Chargers. The longtime Baltimore Colts quarterback left with then-record totals of 2,830 completions, 40,239 yards, and 290 touchdown passes, and a still-record 47 straight games in which he threw at least one touchdown pass.

pounding finally took its toll on a body that had been pushed to full throttle on every play. He was both loved and hated for the mean, take-no-prisoners style he brought to the field, but his success was fueled by a consuming drive to be the best and a relentless dedication to his profession.

The burly Butkus combined surprising speed with a fearsome strength that he used to fight off powerful blockers. A ball carrier who fell into the grasp of his long, thick arms could expect to be squeezed into helpless submission.

Other runners and offensive linemen were constantly amazed by the ferocity of his hits. Butkus could run down ball carriers from sideline to sideline, shadow running backs in pass coverage, and make the right calls for coach George Halas' complicated defense.

Butkus' misfortune was that he played for weak Chicago teams that never challenged for NFL superiority. But he played in eight Pro Bowls, and the notoriety he gained beyond his hometown of Chicago made him a legend. Butkus' incredible instinct for the ball can be documented by the 25 opponents' fumbles he recovered and the 22 interceptions he recorded in 119 professional games. He also is known as one of best ball-stripping tacklers in league history, having the uncanny ability to make a tackle with one arm and knock the ball free with the other.

Monster of the Midway *Middle linebacker Dick Butkus was a ferocious defender for the Chicago Bears in a career that eventually led to the Hall of Fame.*

1974

Day of the Dolphins, Part II

The Miami Dolphins utilized a bulldozing ground attack and a suffocating defense to overwhelm the Minnesota Vikings and win the NFL championship with a 24–7 victory in Super Bowl VIII at Houston on January 13. It was Miami's second consecutive league title, coming on the heels of its perfect season in 1972.

The Dolphins were not perfect during the 1973 season—but they were close. They won 12 of 14 games during the regular portion of the schedule, then routed the Cincinnati Bengals and the Oakland Raiders in the AFC playoffs. The Vikings also won 12 regular-season games, then ousted the Washington Redskins and the Dallas Cowboys in the NFC playoffs to reach the Super Bowl.

Once they reached the league title game, however, the Vikings were no match for the experienced Dolphins. Miami drove 62 and 56 yards to touchdowns the first two times it had the ball, and the Dolphins never looked back. The score was 24–0 before Minnesota scored a touchdown in the fourth quarter.

Burly fullback Larry Csonka of Miami was the game's most valuable player. He carried the ball 33 times for a Super Bowl-record 145 yards as the Dolphins gained 196 of their 259 total yards on the ground. Miami quarterback Bob Griese rarely passed the ball, but when he did, he was efficient. He completed six of seven attempts for 73 yards.

Back-to-Back

The Miami Dolphins became the second team in the short history of the Super Bowl to that time to win back-to-back titles (the Green Bay Packers took games I and II). The complete list of teams with consecutive Super Bowl wins through the 2003 season:

TEAM	GAMES
Green Bay Packers	I and II
Miami Dolphins	VII and VIII
Pittsburgh Steelers	IX and X
Pittsburgh Steelers	XIII and XIV
San Francisco 49ers	XXIII and XXIV
Dallas Cowboys	XXVII and XXVIII
Denver Broncos	XXXII and XXXIII

Note: No club ever has won three consecutive Super Bowls.

There It Goes   *All eyes are on the flight of the ball as Hank Aaron hits his record 715th career home run (page 44).*

College Basketball's Streak Stoppers

Two of college basketball's most amazing streaks came to an end in 1974: the 88-game winning streak of University of California at Los Angeles (UCLA) Bruins, and the same school's seven-year run as NCAA champion.

The Notre Dame Fighting Irish ended UCLA's record winning streak, which began in 1971, with a 71–70 victory in South Bend on January 19. The Bruins appeared well on their way to win number 89 in a row when they held a 70–59 lead with just 3:32 to play. But UCLA did not score again. Meanwhile, the Irish capitalized on five Bruins' turnovers, and took a 71–70 lead when Dwight Clay sank a jumper from the corner with 29 seconds left. UCLA missed five shots at a potential winning basket in the closing seconds, and Notre Dame held on for the one-point victory.

On March 23, UCLA was ousted from the NCAA Tournament by the North

1974

Carolina State Wolfpack in the semifinals—but it took two overtimes to do it. The Wolfpack overcame a seven-point deficit in the second extra session to win 80–77. Then they went on to beat Marquette 76–54 in the title game. For the first time since 1966, college basketball had a new champion.

Baseball's New Home Run King

Atlanta Braves slugger Hank Aaron (b.1954) became baseball's all-time home run leader when he hit his 715th career blast in a game at Atlanta Stadium on April 8. "Hammerin' Hank" belted a fastball from Los Angeles Dodgers left-hander Al Downing over the left-field fence in the fourth inning of the Braves' home opener. Aaron broke legendary Babe Ruth's career mark of 714 home runs, which stood nearly four decades.

The Braves' outfielder had ended the 1973 season at 713 career home runs.

Atlanta opened the 1974 season on the road at Cincinnati, where Aaron tied Ruth's mark with number 714 off the Reds' Jack Billingham on Opening Day. Aaron did not play in the Braves' next game, then failed to homer in the third game, thus giving him a chance to break the record in front of the home fans.

Aaron's historic home run off Downing tied the game at 3–3. The Braves went on to win 7–4.

Celtics Back on Top

It was a tumultuous year in 1974. The Watergate drama paralyzed the country and eventually led to President Richard Nixon's resignation. (Briefly, Nixon and men working for him had tried to cover up a break-in at Democratic Party headquarters; the resulting scandal ended Nixon's presidency and sent several members of his staff to prison.) The energy crisis sapped the nation's spirit. Heiress Patty Hearst's kidnapping was a real-life drama.

In the NBA, though, everything was back to normal. That's right, the Boston Celtics were champions again. Boston, which won 11 league championships from 1957 to 1969, returned to the top after a four-season hiatus. The Celtics won 56 of 82 regular-season games, then breezed past the Buffalo Braves and the New York Knicks in the playoffs before taking a taut, seven-game Finals series against the Milwaukee Bucks. Center Dave Cowens (b.1948) was the star in the decisive game, when he scored 28 points and grabbed 14 rebounds in Boston's 102–87 victory on May 12.

The Daytona 450?

The nation was in the grips of a fuel shortage in 1974, and all Americans were forced to conserve energy, especially in their cars. That included NASCAR, which conserved by shortening races on the early portions of its schedule by 10 percent. Thus, the Daytona 500 on February 17 was just 450 miles.

That made little difference to Richard Petty, who won the race for the fifth time in its 16-year history. He became the first driver to win it in consecutive seasons.

Hammerin' Hank

Hank Aaron approached Babe Ruth's career home run record the same way he approached just about everything in his life: quietly. Aaron always did things at his own pace, and he seemed to view reaching the record as nothing more than a part of his job. The steadiness of his character was reflected in his extraordinary consistency at the plate. For 23 years, Aaron averaged nearly 33 home runs a year, yet he never hit more than 47 in any one season. When he finally retired in 1976, Aaron had 755 career home runs.

It is difficult to separate Aaron's career from its historical context. He began his professional career in 1952 with the Indianapolis Clowns of the Negro League, and his career unfolded along with the civil-rights movement. As a minor leaguer in the Deep South, Aaron encountered racial prejudices that would shadow his career but helped him forge the quiet, dignified approach that was to prove his greatest asset in the Majors.

After he joined the Milwaukee Braves in 1954, Aaron demonstrated the sweet stroke that earned him two batting titles and four home run crowns. Still, many fans were surprised when it became obvious that Aaron was going to break Ruth's record. Some Americans did not want a black man to break the mark, and others could not conceive that someone they perceived as ordinary would eclipse the larger-than-life Ruth. They tainted Aaron's pursuit of the record with hundreds of angry and bigoted letters. Reflecting on the experience, Aaron has said that, although this should have been the most enjoyable time in his life, it was, instead, "hell."

In the end, the letters were about as effective as opposing pitchers. Aaron continued to hit, and the records continued to fall. In addition to the home run record, he set career records for runs batted in and total bases. His final career total of 755 home runs ensures that he will always be included among baseball's all-time greatest players.

Girls Play, Too

 Women and girls continued to make gains in the world of sports.

Girls had played Little League baseball as far back as 1950. Then again, it was a girl disguised as a boy playing in New York State. That situation prompted Little League Baseball to officially ban girls the following year. More than 20 years later, in 1972, Maria Pepe played several games for a team in Hoboken, New Jersey. Little League Baseball refused to lift its ban, however, and the National Organization for Women (NOW) sued. On June 12, a New Jersey court ruled in favor of NOW, and Little League

Baseball opened to girls as well as boys. (Later in the year, Bunny Taylor became the first girl to pitch an official Little League no-hitter.) Today, Little League Baseball boasts that more than 50,000 girls play its game.

Also in 1974, minor-league baseball's Portland Mavericks hired baseball's first female coach, Lanny Moss. The next year, Moss became the general manager of the Northwest League club, which was not affiliated with a Major League team.

By the way, Portland really was a maverick franchise. In 1974, its manager, Frank Peters, orchestrated an unusual stunt. He had his players rotate each inning so that they each played one position

Mixed Doubles *Chris Evert gives a peck on the cheek to fiancee Jimmy Connors at Wimbledon in July. The two stars, who were engaged to be married later in the year, each won singles titles.*

time. A quarterfinalist in both 1972 and 1973, the third-seeded Connors reached the finals this time. He lost only six games while defeating veteran Ken Rosewall (b.1934) in straight sets in the final.

Evert, who reached the semifinals during her debut in 1972 and made it to the finals the following year, beat Russia's Olga Morozova 6–0, 6–4 to win the first of her three Wimbledon singles crowns.

Connors and Evert were engaged to be married in November. Although the engagement eventually was called off, Wimbledon was the background to three other relationships. Bjorn Borg (b.1956) married Romanian player Mariana Simionescu a month after winning his fifth consecutive Wimbledon title in 1980 (they had first met at the French Open four years earlier), and Evert dated another tennis player, Britain's John Lloyd, for the first time at Wimbledon in 1978. They married a year later.

There was, alas, no happy ending for the marriages of Borg and Evert. Both marriages ended in divorce.

during a nine-inning game. It worked, too! The Mavericks won 8–7.

Love Match

Everyone knows Paris is for lovers. So, too, is Wimbledon, even if you are a player. Although in the past Wimbledon honors had occasionally gone to husband and wife or brother and sister teams in the doubles events, true singles romance hit the headlines in 1974. On July 5 and 6, Jimmy Connors (b.1952) and Chris Evert (b.1954) celebrated their engagement by winning the singles titles on Centre Court.

Connors, aged 21, and Evert, 19, were both playing at Wimbledon for the third

Teen Sensation

Moses Malone (b.1954), a 6-foot-11 high school star from Petersburg, Virginia, became the first basketball player to bypass college and go straight to the pros. On August 29, Malone signed a potential $3 million contract with the Utah Stars of the American Basketball Association (ABA).

Malone went on to become one of basketball's all-time great centers. He was a relentless rebounder and effective scorer who played in the pros for 21 seasons.

The third-leading rebounder and fifth-leading scorer in NBA history (the ABA merged with the NBA for the 1976–77 season), he was honored in 1996–97 as a member of the league's 50th Anniversary All-Time Team.

Malone was the NBA's Most Valuable Player in 1979, 1982, and 1983. He teamed with another former ABA star, forward Julius Erving (b.1950), to help the Philadelphia 76ers win the NBA title in 1983.

California Dreamin'

Baseball's World Series was played entirely in California for the first time, with the American League-champion Oakland A's taking on the National League-champion Los Angeles Dodgers. The A's won their third consecutive championship by taking the Series in five games.

Mustachioed relief pitcher Rollie Fingers was the star for Oakland. Fingers won the Series opener, then closed out each of his team's next three victories, including a 3–2 decision in the final game. Oakland batted only .211 in the Series and managed only eight extra-base hits, but one of them was Joe Rudi's home run to break a 2–2 tie in the bottom of the seventh inning of Game 5. Fingers made the run stand up for a 3–2 victory that ended the Series (four of the five games were decided by that same score; the A's won the fourth game 5–2).

Oakland became the first club to win three consecutive World Series since the New York Yankees won five in a row from 1949 to 1953.

Soon after the A's beat the Dodgers in the World Series, star pitcher Catfish Hunter became the first Oakland star to take flight as a free agent; others would follow in subsequent years. The dynasty was already crumbling.

Muhammad Ali Plays Rope-a-Dope

Former heavyweight boxing champion Muhammad Ali (b.1942) made his mark as a dancer in the ring, often taunting his opponents to come after him. He'd "float like a butterfly," as he liked to put it. But on October 29, in the "Rumble in the Jungle" in Zaire against George Foreman (b.1949), the reigning champ, Ali dramatically changed his tactics.

For most of the early rounds, Ali backed up to the ropes and let Foreman flail away. Foreman was known for his powerful punches, but his shots fell harmlessly against Ali's arms. By the eighth round, the champion was exhausted. Ali, sensing his chance, went on the offensive and knocked Foreman out.

The stunning strategy made Ali the heavyweight champion for a second time. In 1967, he had his title stripped after he refused induction into military service.

Trojan Horse

University of Southern California (USC) Trojans running back Anthony Davis already had made his mark in his team's storied rivalry against the Notre Dame Fighting Irish when he scored six touchdowns in a 45–23 victory in 1972. But he and his teammates earned a

1974

permanent place in their school's football lore with an unbelievable comeback on November 30 at the Los Angeles Memorial Coliseum.

The sixth-ranked Trojans were being pasted by the fifth-rated Irish, who sported the nation's number-one defense, 24–0 late in the second quarter. Only seconds before halftime, though, Davis caught a short touchdown pass from quarterback Pat Haden. Then he opened the second half with an electrifying 100-yard kickoff return for a touchdown that sent the crowd into a frenzy. Davis scored two more touchdowns in the third quarter to put USC ahead, and his teammates took it

from there. By the time the Trojans' scoring burst was over early in the fourth quarter, they had amassed a remarkable 55 points in just 17 minutes of game action. Their 55–24 victory helped spur the Trojans to college football's national championship for 1974.

The End of One Dynasty . . .

The Miami Dolphins' string of three consecutive AFC titles and their bid for a third consecutive Super Bowl championship ended when Oakland Raiders running back Clarence Davis made a miraculous catch to give his team a 28–26 victory in a divisional playoff game at Oakland on December 21.

The Raiders and Dolphins played a thrilling game that saw the lead change hands five times in the second half. Miami appeared to keep its drive to another Super Bowl alive when Benny Malone ran 23 yards for a touchdown and a 26–21 lead with just 2:08 remaining. But Oakland quickly marched down the field. The Raiders reached the Dolphins' eight-yard line, where quarterback Ken Stabler was about to be sacked before he flipped a pass to Davis, who was amidst three Miami players in the end zone. Somehow, Davis grabbed it for the winning touchdown with 26 seconds left.

"That was my toughest loss in coaching," Miami's Don Shula (b.1930) said afterward.

The game marked the end of the Dolphins' dynasty. The next season, star running backs Larry Csonka and Jim Kiick, plus future Hall of Fame wide receiver Paul Warfield, bolted to the World Football

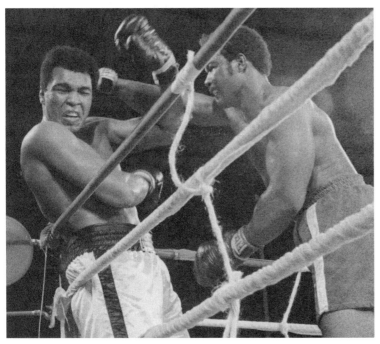

On the Ropes *Challenger Muhammad Ali let champion George Foreman hammer away in the early rounds of their heavyweight title bout. Then Ali knocked out the weary Foreman in the eighth round.*

Other Milestones of 1974

✔ On February 15, hockey great Phil Esposito scored the 1,000th point of his NHL career.

✔ Speedster Ivory Crockett ran the 100-yard dash in nine seconds flat to set a new world record during a meet in Knoxville, Tennessee, on May 11.

✔ Goalie Bernie Parent fashioned a 1–0 shutout of the high-scoring Boston Bruins on May 19 in Philadelphia to lead the hometown Flyers to the NHL's Stanley Cup title.

✔ The University of Southern California (USC) Trojans capped an unprecedented string of five consecutive NCAA titles in baseball by beating Miami (Florida) 7–3 in the final game of the College World Series in Omaha in June. Through 2003, USC had a record 12 titles.

✔ The first commercially sponsored beach volleyball tournament took place in San Diego, California in the summer of 1974. Winston Cigarettes was the event's title sponsor.

✔ St. Louis Cardinals outfielder Lou Brock stole a big-league-record 118 bases. He shattered the old mark of 104, set by Maury Wills in 1962.

✔ The Birmingham Americans defeated the Florida Blazers 22–21 on December 5 to win the first championship of the World Football League.

✔ On December 20, a federal judge ruled that the NFL's player reserve system was illegal. The ruling opened the door for eventual free agency in pro football.

Lou Brock

League (they had signed with the WFL's Toronto Northmen in March, but played out their Miami contracts). Miami missed the playoffs in 1975 for the first time since 1969.

. . . The Beginning of Another Dynasty

Just as one dynasty was ending in Miami, another was beginning in Pittsburgh, where the Steelers qualified for their first Super Bowl by beating the Oakland Raiders 24–13 in the AFC Championship Game on December 29.

Even as several significant NFL rules changes opened up offenses around the league, the Steelers' defense proved to be remarkably stingy. Led by future Pro Football Hall of Famers such as defensive tackle "Mean Joe" Greene, linebacker Jack Lambert, and cornerback Mel Blount, the "Steel Curtain" allowed opponents an average of only 13.5 points per game, and the Steelers permitted the fewest yards in the league.

1975

It's a Happy New Year for USC

The University of Southern California (USC) Trojans won a thrilling, 18–17 decision over the Ohio State Buckeyes in the Rose Bowl in Pasadena, California, on New Year's Day. The next day, the Trojans found out that the victory had propelled them to a share of college football's national championship.

The Trojans had little reason to believe they had a chance at the title after finishing the regular season 9–1–1 and ranked fifth in the country. But they beat the third-ranked Buckeyes when Pat Haden lofted a 38-yard touchdown pass to John McKay late in the game, then Shelton Diggs followed with a diving catch of a two-point conversion pass.

That night, top-ranked Alabama was upset by Notre Dame in the Orange Bowl, and the Trojans vaulted to number one in the United Press International poll. The Associated Press champion already had been determined before the bowls. The Oklahoma Sooners breezed to an 11–0 record and the title. But the school was on probation and ineligible to play in a bowl game or compete for the UPI crown.

The Steelers Win Their First NFL Title

There were tears in NFL commissioner Pete Rozelle's (1926–1996) eyes when he presented the Vince Lombardi Trophy to Pittsburgh Steelers owner Art Rooney (1901–1988) in the locker room following Super Bowl IX in New Orleans on January 12. "No man ever deserved it more," Rozelle said. Rooney's Steelers had just beaten the Minnesota Vikings 16–6 at Tulane Stadium, giving Pittsburgh its first league championship.

The 73-year-old Rooney had founded the franchise in 1933 and had been at the club's helm for all but a brief period during the 1940s. But the Steelers (who were called the Pirates, the same as Pittsburgh's baseball team, until 1940) enjoyed little success in their first four decades. They didn't have a winning season until 1942 and reached the postseason just once—they lost a divisional playoff in 1947—until 1972. They won a club record 11 games that year, however, advanced in the playoffs when Franco Harris made a miraculous catch to beat the Oakland Raiders, and began a string of eight consecutive playoff appearances.

Hail to the Chief *Steelers owner Art Rooney, also known as the "Chief," accepts the Vince Lombardi Trophy from NFL commissioner Pete Rozelle for winning the Super Bowl.*

It was the Steelers' defense that carried the club to its first Super Bowl appearance. Once there, the "Steel Curtain" didn't let up. Pittsburgh permitted the Vikings only 119 total yards (just 17 of them on the ground), intercepted three passes, recovered two fumbles, and recorded a safety. Minnesota's lone points came on a blocked punt that was recovered in the end zone for a touchdown.

On offense, Pittsburgh running back Franco Harris carried 34 times for 158 yards and was named the game's most valuable player.

1975

The Perfect Going-Away Present

After his University of California at Los Angeles (UCLA) Bruins edged Louisville 75–74 in overtime in the NCAA men's basketball tournament semifinals on March 29, head coach John Wooden (b.1910) announced his retirement. The "Wizard of Westwood," who won more than 80 percent of his games in 27 years as a college coach, decided that the title game against the Kentucky Wildcats on March 31 in San Diego would be his last.

The Bruins' players sent their coach out in style. With center Richard Washington (28 points) and forward Dave Meyers (24 points) combining for 52 points, UCLA beat the Wildcats 92–85. It was the Bruins' 10th national championship in 12 seasons.

Women in the Sports Headlines

Title IX—the landmark ruling that prohibits institutions that receive federal funding from discriminating against women in educational programs or athletic activities—originally was written in 1972 but officially went into effect on June 21 of this year. With or without Title IX, however, women were making big headlines in sports in 1975:

- Women's college basketball powers Immaculata and Queens played at Madison Square Garden on January 27. It was a first at the Garden and drew nearly 12,000 fans. Immaculata won 65–61.

- American distance runner Francie Larrieu, who already held several world indoor records, set another in the 1,500 meters in a race in Toronto on February 14.

- Dorothy Hamill won the second of her three consecutive United States figure skating championships. She eventually would complete an impressive triple in 1976 with a world figure skating title and an Olympic gold medal (see page 61).

- Chris Evert outlasted Evonne Goolagong-Cawley in three sets to win the U.S. Open tennis championship for the first time at Forest Hills in September. Evert began a string of four consecutive national titles.

Frank Robinson Manages to Break a Color Barrier

Frank Robinson (b.1935) became the first African-American to manage a Major League Baseball team when he took the reins of the Cleveland Indians for the 1975 season. Actually, the superstar outfielder (he won baseball's Triple Crown in 1966 when he led the American League in batting average, home runs, and RBI) and designated hitter had been named the Indians' player-manager back on October 3, 1974, at the conclusion of the previous season. But his on-field debut came in the 1975 season opener against the New York Yankees on April 8.

Robinson the manager penciled in Robinson the designated hitter into the lineup that day. And in his first at bat in the first inning, he belted a solo home run off New York's Doc Medich. Robinson's blast helped the Indians beat the Yankees 5–3 in his debut. Cleveland struggled, however, to a 79–80 record and a fourth-place finish in the American League East by season's end.

The Warriors Win the NBA Title

The Golden State Warriors, with a cast that featured superstar forward Rick Barry (b.1944) teamed with a host of supporting players, stunned the heavily favored Washington Bullets in the NBA Finals. Golden State swept the series in four games.

Barry ranked among the league leaders in scoring (at 30.6 points per game, he was second only to Buffalo's Bob McAdoo) and assists (6.2 per game, which was sixth) during the regular season while leading the Warriors to the Pacific Division title. But they won a relatively modest 48 of 82 games, and were decided underdogs against a Bullets' team that won 60 times and waltzed to the Central Division championship by 19 games. "No one took us very seriously," Warriors head coach Al Attles said.

As expected, the Finals did turn out to be a mismatch—but in Golden State's favor. Though the games were close, the Warriors took each of the first three games. By Game Four on May 25, the Bullets were so frustrated that guard Mike Riordan nearly tackled Barry early on in what the Warriors believed was an attempt to get the volatile superstar tossed from the game. Barry kept his cool, though, and the Warriors went on to win 96–95. Barry was named the most valuable player of the Finals after averaging 29.5 points per game.

One footnote to the series: For the first time in major sports history in this country, both head coaches in a championship matchup (the Warriors' Attles, and

Another Barrier Broken *Frank Robinson became the first African-American manager in the big leagues when he took over the Cleveland Indians (see page 52).*

the Bullets' K.C. Jones) were African-American. It was a tribute to the diversity of the NBA, however, that this was only a footnote, and not a major media story.

All Four None

For the first time in baseball history, four pitchers combined on a no-hitter during the Oakland A's 5–0 victory over the California Angels on the last day of baseball's regular season. More than 22,000 fans were on hand at the Oakland-Alameda County Coliseum on September 28 when the A's, who were

53

1975

readying themselves for the playoffs, made history.

Vida Blue started and pitched five hitless innings before giving way to reliever Glenn Abbott. He didn't allow a hit in the sixth, and neither did Paul Lindblad in the seventh. Closer Rollie Fingers shut the door in the eighth and ninth innings.

Ali Outslugs Frazier in a "Thrilla"

Thirty-something boxing greats Muhammad Ali and Joe Frazier (b.1944) stepped into the ring in Manila on October 1 and delighted a large crowd that included Philippine President Ferdinand Marcos with an exciting bout. Ali eventually defended his heavyweight crown when Frazier could not come out of his corner for the 15th round.

Ali and Frazier had split two prior meetings in the ring. Frazier won the first, a unanimous 15-round decision in 1971 in New York's Madison Square Garden to defend his title and hand Ali his first loss in 32 fights. Ali came back to win the rematch, a non-title bout also in New York

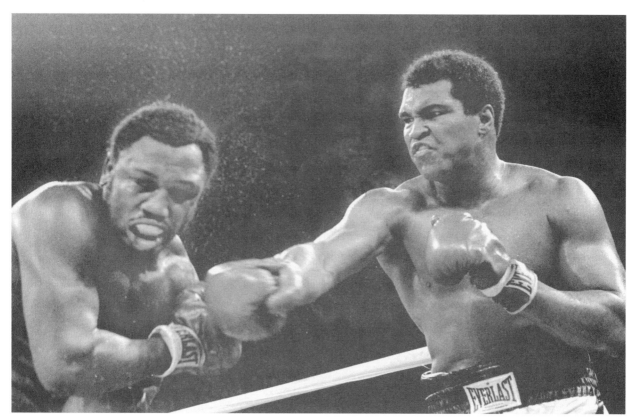

Rubber Match *Muhammad Ali (right) made it two out of three against Joe Frazier in the "Thrilla in Manila."*

in 1974 to earn a shot at champion George Foreman (see page 47).

In this one, Ali and Frazier slugged it out toe-to-toe right from the start. Frazier, the title challenger, had the upper hand in the middle rounds. "I hit him with punches that would bring down the walls of a city," Frazier said. But Ali stood his ground, then closed with a flourish, pummeling his opponent the final three rounds. By the end of the 14th round, Frazier was visibly exhausted, and his manager threw in the towel. The championship fight has come to be known as the "Thrilla in Manila."

Prior to beating Frazier, Ali also defended his heavyweight crown in 1975 against challengers Chuck Wepner (in Richfield, Ohio, on March 24) and Joe Bugner (in Malaysia on July 1).

The Reds Win a Fall Classic

The Cincinnati Reds beat the Boston Red Sox 4–3 in the seventh and deciding game of the World Series October 22 at Boston's Fenway Park. Thus, the Reds outlasted the Red Sox four games to three in what is widely regarded as one of the greatest World Series ever.

Boston went home for Game Six on October 21 trailing three games to two. The next two games packed enough drama to keep baseball fans talking about the Series to this day. First, the Red Sox clawed their way from the brink of elimination by winning the sixth game 7–6 in 12 innings. Boston trailed 6–3 until pinch-hitter Bernie Carbo launched a three-run home run to tie the game in the bottom of the eighth inning. The Red Sox squandered a

(see page 47).

The Curse of the Bambino

Pitcher-outfielder Babe Ruth (1895–1948) helped the Boston Red Sox win three World Series titles in four seasons from 1915 to 1918. But after the 1919 season, Ruth was sold to the New York Yankees to help owner Harry Frazee cover mounting theatrical losses. That watershed deal proved to put the two franchises at a crossroads of epic proportions.

Before acquiring Ruth, the Yankees had not won a World Series. But Ruth turned the franchise into a power, and its 26 world championships are far and away the most in baseball history.

Before trading Ruth, the Red Sox's five World Series titles were more than any other team in baseball. They haven't won a World Series since. Each of the four times Boston has reached the Fall Classic since then, the Red Sox have lost in seven games.

none-out, bases-loaded opportunity in the bottom of the ninth, but relievers Dick Drago and Rick Wise held the Reds scoreless through the 12th. Drago got a big assist in the 11th inning from right fielder Dwight Evans, who went into the stands to snatch a potential go-ahead home run away from Cincinnati second baseman Joe Morgan.

In the bottom of the 12th, Boston catcher Carlton Fisk blasted a solo homer to end the game. The dramatic television footage of Fisk anxiously watching his long drive, arms raised, waving the ball to stay fair, is one of baseball's most memorable scenes ever.

Fisk's heroics carried the Red Sox to the brink of their first world championship since 1918 (see box). But Boston could not shut the door on the Reds in Game Seven despite taking a 3–0 lead early on. First baseman Tony Perez narrowed Cincinnati's deficit to one run with a two-run home run in the sixth inning, and the Reds tied it with another run in

1975

the seventh. In the top of the ninth inning, Morgan blooped a single to center field to plate Ken Griffey with the winning run. Reliever Will McEnaney retired the Red Sox in order in the bottom of the ninth to save it, and the "Big Red Machine," which had won 108 games during the regular season, captured the franchise's first World Series since 1940.

Archie Griffin Doubles His Fun

 For its first 40 years, the Heisman Trophy (given annually to the na-tion's premier college football player) had been awarded to 40 different players. But on December 2 at the Downtown Athletic Club in New York City, Ohio State running back Archie Griffin became the first player ever to win the award twice.

Griffin finished his college career with a then-record 5,176 rushing yards (the mark would last only one year before Pittsburgh's Tony Dorsett shattered it). Before Griffin in 1974, four juniors—Army fullback Doc Blanchard (1945), SMU halfback Doak Walker (1948), Ohio State halfback Vic Janowicz (1950) and Navy quarterback Roger Staubach (1963)—had

Body English *Boston Red Sox catcher Carlton Fisk pleads for his long fly to stay fair in game six of the World Series. It did, though Cincinnati won the Series the next night.*

Other Milestones of 1975

✔ Golfer Jack Nicklaus drained a 40-foot birdie putt on the 16th hole to help give him his fifth Masters title on April 13.

✔ The Philadelphia Flyers defeated the Buffalo Sabres in six games in the NHL finals to win their second consecutive Stanley Cup.

✔ Distance-running star Steve Prefontaine died at 24 in a car accident in Eugene, Oregon on May 30.

✔ California Angels pitcher Nolan Ryan equaled Sandy Koufax's big-league record by tossing his fourth career no-hitter. Ryan shut down the Baltimore Orioles 1–0 on June 1.

✔ International soccer star Pele signed with the North American Soccer League's New York Cosmos. Pele debuted in an exhibition against the Dallas Tornados on June 15.

✔ Two firsts for men's and women's tennis: Players at the Wimbledon tournament that concluded in July were allowed to rest on chairs during changeovers, and lights were installed to accommodate night matches at Forest Hills for the U.S. Open that concluded in September.

Pele

✔ The World Football League failed in its challenge to the established NFL, folding in October before it could complete its second season.

✔ An arbitrator's ruling December 23 opened the door for widespread baseball free agency in later years and, subsequently, skyrocketing salaries. Labor arbitrator Peter Seitz ruled that pitchers Andy Messersmith and Dave McNally were free to sign with any team. McNally retired, but Messersmith went on to play for three teams the next four seasons.

---

won the coveted Heisman. But Griffin was the first, and still only, player to duplicate the feat as a senior.

Staubach's Prayer Is Answer

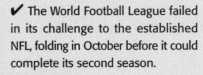 With his team trailing the Minnesota Vikings 14–10 and time running out in an NFC Divisional Playoff Game in Bloomington on December 28, Dallas Cowboys quarterback Roger Staubach (b.1942) dropped back to pass from midfield and heaved the ball as far as he could. "I closed my eyes and said a Hail Mary," Staubach told reporters in the locker room afterward.

Staubach's prayer was answered. Cowboys wide receiver Drew Pearson caught the ball at the five-yard line, cradling the ball on his hip despite close coverage from a pair of Vikings' defenders. He fell into the end zone with 24 seconds left to give the Cowboys a 17–14 victory.

A desperation heave at the end of football games has been around a long time, of course. But Staubach's miracle officially launched its designation as a "Hail Mary pass."

1976

The Buckeyes Are Foiled Again

The Ohio State Buckeyes, undefeated and ranked number one in the nation, had their national-championship hopes derailed by the upstart University of California at Los Angeles (UCLA) Bruins in the Rose Bowl in Pasadena, California, on New Year's Day. UCLA won the game 23–10.

The Buckeyes had rolled to 11 consecutive victories entering the New Year, but they managed only a 3–0 halftime lead against the Bruins despite dominating the first two quarters. That seemed to inspire UCLA, which opened up a 16–3 advantage in the third quarter, largely on the strength of two touchdown passes from quarterback John Sciarra to wide receiver Wally Henry. Running back Wendell Tyler's 54-yard touchdown run in the fourth quarter sealed the outcome.

It was another bitter setback for head coach Woody Hayes (1913–1987) and his Buckeyes. On New Year's Day 1975, Ohio State could have earned a share of the national championship, only to lose a heartbreaking decision to the University of Southern California, which earned the title. This time, the beneficiary of Ohio State's misfortune was Oklahoma University, which ascended to the top of the polls with a 14–6 victory over Michigan in the Orange Bowl.

The Flyers Bully Their Way Past the Soviets

Off the ice, diplomatic relations between the United States and the Soviet Union were still frosty with the Cold War ongoing in the mid-1970s. On the ice, the rivalry between the two countries would escalate until the United States' memorable "Miracle on Ice" victory during the 1980 Winter Olympics. But the Philadelphia Flyers' win in a 1976 exhibition against the Soviet Central Army team on January 11 heightened tensions on both fronts.

The Flyers, hockey's reigning Stanley Cup champions, beat the Soviets 4–1 in an international exhibition at the Spectrum in Philadelphia. The game probably would have been merely a footnote except for the stark contrast between the intimidation tactics of the "Broad Street Bullies," as the Flyers had come to be known, and the finesse of the Soviet team—it was a

World's Greatest Athlete *Bruce Jenner earned that distinction after winning the Olympic decathlon (see page 63).*

difference that nearly resulted in the game's forfeiture.

Midway through the first period, Soviet star Valery Kharlamov was sent to the ice with a hit from behind by a Flyers' defenseman. The Soviet coach pulled his team from the rink. NHL officials and members of the Soviet delegation huddled. Sixteen minutes later, the Soviets returned to the ice—but a man short because of a delay-of-game penalty they were issued. The Flyers quickly scored on a power play and breezed to victory.

The Steelers Win Another Super Bowl

The Pittsburgh Steelers edged the Dallas Cowboys 21–17 in a thrilling Super Bowl played at the Orange Bowl in Miami on January 18. The Cowboys led a tense, defensive battle 10–7 in the fourth quarter before the Steelers took command by scoring 14 points in unusual fashion: on a safety, two field goals and a touchdown (while missing the extra point).

Richard Petty: The King

Richard Petty may have lost the Daytona 500 in a wild finish in 1976, but that hardly tarnished his crown. He'll forever be known as "The King" to NASCAR fans around the country.

Petty, the son of Hall of Fame driver Lee Petty, won his first NASCAR title in 1964. Then he left little doubt that he was destined to be known as one of the greatest drivers of all time with a dominating season in 1967. That year, he won an unbelievable 27 of the 48 races he entered, including 10 in a row in one stretch.

In a 35-yard career from 1958 to 1992, Petty won a record 200 races—nearly double the total of David Pearson's runnerup 105. Petty also holds all-time NASCAR records for the most career starts, poles, top-five finishes and top-10 finishes, and he shares the mark for the most season championships (he and Dale Earnhardt, Sr. each won seven titles).

But Petty's influence goes well beyond the statistics. He is arguably the most popular driver in NASCAR history, and his trademark grin beneath a cowboy hat and dark sunglasses is recognized around the country even by non-racing fans. He remains a popular product spokesman more than a decade after his retirement from competitive racing. He's hardly retired altogether, however, because he remains active with Petty Enterprises, a car owner on the current NASCAR circuit.

The safety came when Pittsburgh backup running back Reggie Harrison blocked a punt out of the end zone early in the fourth quarter to trim the Steelers' deficit to one point. After Roy Gerela kicked field goals of 36 yards and 18 yards to give Pittsburgh a 15–10 advantage, Steelers wide receiver Lynn Swann (b.1952) hauled in a 64-yard touchdown pass from Terry Bradshaw (b.1948) for the clinching touchdown with 3:02 remaining. The Cowboys closed within four points with a late touchdown, then held the Steelers on downs, but safety Glen Edwards sealed Pittsburgh's second consecutive Super Bowl win with an interception in the end zone on the final play.

Swann's fourth-quarter touchdown capped a brilliant day. He caught just four passes, but they went for 161 yards and earned him the game's most valuable player award. His ballet-like, 53-yard, fingertip grab in the second quarter is one of most remarkable catches in NFL history.

While the game turned on Harrison's blocked punt, the most important play may actually have been a failed field-goal attempt in the third quarter. With his team trailing by only three points, Gerela misfired on a 36-yard try. Dallas safety Cliff Harris mocked him by applauding the miss and patting him on the helmet. That bit of gamesmanship infuriated Steelers linebacker Jack Lambert, who tossed Harris to the ground.

"The Pittsburgh Steelers aren't supposed to be intimidated," Lambert growled afterward. "We're supposed to do the intimidating. I decided to do something about it."

Momentum swung to Pittsburgh's side, and the Steelers controlled the action much of the way after that.

David Pearson Crawls Across the Finish Line

In one of the most bizarre, yet exciting, NASCAR finishes ever, David Pearson inched across the finish line to edge Richard Petty (b.1937) and win the prestigious Daytona 500 stock-car race on February 15.

Pearson and Petty often raced side-by-side toward the checkered flag throughout their careers. Pearson, in fact, won more career races than anyone else in NASCAR history—anyone else except Petty, that is. They called Petty "The King," and for good reason (see the box on the opposite page). He won 200 races in all. This one got away from him on the last lap, however.

Petty was in front until Pearson sped by on the backstretch. That was no problem for The King, who immediately dove down inside to try to retake the lead. For a short time, the legendary drivers zoomed side-by-side, pedal to the metal. But coming out of the last turn, the two cars bumped. Pearson went careening into the wall. Petty spun wildly, then started going backwards toward the finish line before his car gave out only 50 yards from the end.

Pearson, meanwhile, bounced off the wall and hit another car, keeping him on the track. His front end was mangled, but his car still worked. He slowly headed toward the finish line while Petty frantically tried to get his car started again. "It took forever to get there," Pearson said. Eventually, he did. And the checkered flag went to a car that limped home at less than 20 miles per hour—a stark contrast to the day's average speed of 152.181 miles per hour.

Winter Olympics

Dorothy Hamill, a 19-year-old from Riverside, Connecticut, won the gold medal in women's figure skating at the 1976 Winter Olympic Games at Innsbruck, Austria. She also won over the hearts of Americans with her charm, beauty and emotion.

Hamill and speed skater Sheila Young, who won three medals, were the American stars of the Winter Games. Hamill's gold medal was punctuated by dozens of flowers tossed on the ice by admiring fans.

Fender Bender *David Pearson's front end is damaged, but he still manages to cross the finish line and win the Daytona 500 after a last-lap crash with Richard Petty.*

1976

Medal Leaders: Winter Olympics

	GOLD	SILVER	BRONZE	TOTAL
Soviet Union	13	6	8	27
E. Germany	7	5	7	19
United States	3	3	4	10
W. Germany	2	5	3	10
Norway	3	3	1	7
Finland	2	4	1	7

She fought tears before several young girls helped her gather the flowers, and again when the gold medal was placed around her neck. "I probably remember most all the flowers raining down at the end of my performance," she said. "It was quite a shock and a warm feeling."

The gold medalist's signature wedge haircut soon was named for her as young women all over the country went to their stylists to request a "Dorothy Hamill."

Flag Day in Los Angeles

In the midst of the United States' year-long bicentennial celebration, Chicago Cubs star Rick Monday became a contemporary hero. Monday grabbed an American flag from two men who were trying to set it on fire in the outfield at Dodger Stadium during a game on April 25.

Monday had taken his position in center field for the fourth inning when he noticed the men come out of the stands in possession of the flag. Once he realized what they were trying to do, he sprinted toward them and snatched the flag before their lighter could set it on fire. "They couldn't see me coming from behind, but I could see that one had lit a match," Monday said.

Monday safely delivered the flag to the bullpen, and the trespassers were arrested. Ironically, the outfielder was traded to the Dodgers the following year and played in Los Angeles for the last eight seasons of his 19-year, big-league career.

Lucky 13 for the Celtics

The Boston Celtics outlasted the Phoenix Suns in six games to win an NBA Finals series that featured one of the greatest contests in league history. It came in Game Five with the teams tied at two apiece. The Celtics outlasted the Suns 128–126 in three overtimes at the Boston Garden on June 4. After that, Boston's 87–80 victory in Phoenix two days later was almost anticlimactic. Boston's championship was its second in three seasons and its NBA-record 13th overall.

Over in the ABA, the New York Nets won the final title of the league's nine-year existence. The ABA was down to seven teams by the end of the 1976 season. Four of them—the Nets, Denver Nuggets, Indiana Pacers and San Antonio Spurs—officially joined the NBA on June 17.

Before the start of the following NBA season, flashy forward Julius Erving (b.1950), the Nets' superstar, was traded to the Philadelphia 76ers. Erving, who was involved in a contract dispute with the Nets' owner, was sold to Philadelphia for $3 million on October 21. He signed a $3 million deal with his new club.

The Summer Olympics

Decathlete Bruce Jenner (b.1949), swimmers John Naber and Shirley Babashoff, and the American boxing team stood out in an otherwise lackluster Summer Olympic Games for the United States in Montreal. Jenner earned the distinction as the World's Greatest Athlete when he set a world record for points in the 10-event track and field competition. Naber and Babashoff each won five medals (four of Naber's were gold and four of Babashoff's were silver), while the boxers combined for five golds.

After winning his gold medal, Jenner jogged around the Olympic Stadium track carrying an American flag. He quickly became a household name who was in great demand as a product endorser and television personality. Sugar Ray Leonard (see page 89) and brothers Leon and Michael Spinks (see Leon's victory over Muhammad Ali on page 75) all went on to become professional boxing champions.

Overall, the Montreal Games were dominated by the squad from the Soviet Union, while East Germany also had a strong presence. The biggest star of these Olympics, however, may have been one of the smallest competitors. Fourteen-year-old Nadia Comaneci (b.1961), a gymnast from Romania, won three gold medals and delighted fans around the world.

Bedlam in the Bronx

New York Yankees first baseman Chris Chambliss sent the hometown fans into a frenzy with a dramatic, pennant-winning home run in the bottom of the ninth inning of the fifth and final game of the American League Championship Series against the Kansas City Royals on October 14. The teams were tied at two games apiece and were even at 6–6 in Game Five when Chambliss stepped in to face Kansas City reliever Mark Littell to open the last of the ninth.

Chambliss belted Littell's first pitch into the right-field bleachers, touching off a wild celebration at Yankee Stadium. New York fans had grown accustomed to seeing their Yankees win pennants almost at will over the years. But New York's 11-season drought from 1965 to 1975 was its longest since winning its first American League title in 1921. And so, when Chambliss' blast cleared the wall, thousands poured onto the field in celebration. Chambliss, in fact, was knocked to the ground by overzealous fans between second and third base. "I was in the middle of a mass of people, and when I fell to the ground, it was scary," he said. Chambliss was shuffled off the clubhouse, then returned later to touch home plate.

Medal Leaders: Summer Olympics

	GOLD	SILVER	BRONZE	TOTAL
Soviet Union	49	41	35	125
United States	34	35	25	94
E. Germany	40	25	25	90
W. Germany	10	12	17	39
Romania	4	9	14	27

1976

The Big Red Machine Rolls On

While Chris Chambliss' dramatic home run delivered a pennant to New York, the world championship trophy remained in Cincinnati for another season. The Reds had little trouble dispatching the Yankees in four games in the World Series.

Cincinnati second baseman Joe Morgan (b.1943) homered in the bottom of the first inning of Game One, and the

Reds never looked back. The Yankees in fact, led only once in the Series, when they took a 1–0 lead in the first inning of the fourth, and final, game on October 21. Cincinnati erased that deficit with three runs of its own in the fourth inning and went on to win 7–2.

Reds catcher Johnny Bench (b.1947) was the star of the World Series, batting .533 with two home runs and six runs batted in. Bench, arguably the greatest hitting catcher of all time (Mike Piazza fans may disagree), was coming off one of

Heisman Look *Pittsburgh's Tony Dorsett follows a block during his big day against Penn State (see page 65).*

Other Milestones of 1976

✔ Darryl Sittler of the Toronto Maple Leafs scored an NHL-record 10 points in one game against the Boston Bruins on February 7. Sittler scored six goals and had four assists in the Maple Leafs' 11–4 rout.

✔ The Indiana Hoosiers blasted Michigan 86–68 in the final game of the NCAA men's basketball tournament on March 29 to cap a perfect 32–0 season.

✔ Free-agent pitcher Andy Messersmith signed a "lifetime" contract with the Atlanta Braves on April 10. But he lasted only two seasons with the club.

✔ Philadelphia Phillies slugger Mike Schmidt homered in four consecutive at-bats in his team's 18–16 victory over the Chicago Cubs on April 17.

✔ At the Spring Nationals on June 13, Shirley Muldowney became the first woman to win a National Hot Rod Association event.

The Indiana Hoosiers

✔ The last home run of Hank Aaron's career (it was his 755th) came while the all-time home-run king was playing for the Milwaukee Brewers against the California Angels on July 20. Aaron's final blast came off Angels righthander Dick Drago.

---

the poorest offensive seasons of his career. The hitting star during the regular season for Cincinnati was Morgan. The second baseman hit .320 with 27 home runs, 111 runs batted in and 60 steals, and earned his second consecutive National League Most Valuable Player award.

Tony Dorsett Rewrites the Record Book

University of Pittsburgh Panthers running back Tony Dorsett (b.1954) tore through the NCAA record book while leading his team to an unbeaten regular season. Dorsett, a senior, rushed for 1,948 yards in Pittsburgh's 11 victories. He capped the year by running for 224 yards

and two touchdowns in a 24–7 victory over Panthers' rival Penn State on November 26.

That prolific outburst brought Dorsett's career total to an NCAA-record 6,082 rushing yards (he broke the record set by Ohio State's Archie Griffin the previous year; Dorsett's mark would stand until Texas' Ricky Williams broke it in 1998). Dorsett became the first player to rush for more than 1,000 yards all four years of his career, and he tied the mark for the most career touchdowns with 59.

Dorsett, who would go on to a Hall of Fame career in the NFL, was named the Heisman Trophy winner on November 30 as college football's most outstanding player.

1977

Silver and Black Attack

The Oakland Raiders extended the Minnesota Vikings' frustration in the Super Bowl with a convincing 32–14 romp in Super Bowl XI at the Rose Bowl in Pasadena, California, on January 9. Minnesota, which had established itself as one of pro football's dominant teams over the past decade, went 11–2–1 during the regular season to win its fourth consecutive division title and its eighth in nine seasons. But the Vikings lost the Super Bowl for the fourth time in as many tries.

Fred Biletnikoff (b.1943) was the unsung star for Oakland. The quiet wide receiver caught just four passes for 79 yards in the Super Bowl, but three of his receptions directly led to touchdowns. He was named the game's most valuable player. Running back Clarence Davis gained 137 yards to help the Raiders amass a game-record 429 total yards.

Oakland won 13 of 14 games during the regular season to coast to the AFC West title. The Raiders survived a scare from the New England Patriots in the divisional playoffs before routing the Pittsburgh Steelers in the conference title game to reach the Super Bowl.

Courageous Effort

Before there was CNN or AOL Time Warner, before his unprecedented billion-dollar gift to the United Nations, before he married actress Jane Fonda, Ted Turner (b.1938) made headlines by guiding *Courageous* to victory in the America's Cup yacht race in January.

Because Turner had lost in the defender trials aboard *Mariner* three years earlier, some observers feared the bombastic owner of cable superstation TBS and the Atlanta Braves baseball team would become the first skipper to lose the United States' 126-year stranglehold on the America's Cup. But the 39-year-old was an experienced sailor who would earn national Yachtsman of the Year honors four times, and he easily carried *Courageous* to a four-race sweep of challenger Australia in the 1977 finals.

Turner was more successful piloting *Courageous* than he was as the Atlanta Braves' skipper the same year. After a 16-game losing streak prompted Turner to send incumbent manager Dave Bristol on paid leave, Turner stepped into the dugout to manage the club against the Pittsburgh Pirates on May 11. Atlanta lost

Thumbs Up *Atlanta Braves owner Ted Turner also was an experienced sailor who won the America's Cup.*

2–1 to extend its losing streak to 17 games, and National League president Chub Feeney, citing a rule that prohibited managers from owning any part of a club, ordered Turner out of the dugout the next day. Vern Benson took over, and the Braves ended their long losing streak. Turner's career managerial record remains, for all time, 0–1.

Crosby's Last Clambake

Legendary singer Bing Crosby (1903–1977) hosted his last Clambake—the popular professional-amateur

golf tournament in Pebble Beach, California—in January. The internationally renowned entertainer passed away in October after suffering a massive heart attack following a round of golf in Madrid, Spain.

Tom Watson (b.1949) won the Clambake with a tournament-record score of 273 for four rounds. The field was notable for two women whom Crosby invited to participate: Nancy Lopez (b.1957) and Marianne Bretton. They were the first women to play in the tournament since 1939. Another amateur in the field was former President Gerald Ford, whose

1977

errant drives kept gallery patrons on their toes.

Crosby originally started the Clambake (which was officially known as the Crosby National Pro-Am Tournament) in 1937 as a way to get together with friends and raise some money for charity. Until his death, the tournament never lost its casual atmosphere.

Although Crosby's name is no longer associated with the tournament, and corporate sponsorship has diluted some of the camaraderie of the Clambake, the event at Pebble Beach remains one of the most popular stops on the PGA Tour more than a quarter century after his death.

Tears of Joy for Al Maguire

When Al Maguire (1928–2001) announced in January that he was stepping down as Marquette University's head coach after 12 years, effective at the end of the season, he could not have envisioned the drama that still awaited him.

Maguire's Warriors lost seven games during the regular season and were one of the last teams to make it into the NCAA tournament (which at the time included only 32 teams—half the current total). But Marquette beat University of Cincinnati convincingly in the opening round of the March tournament, survived a one-point scare against Kansas State University, then upset Wake Forest University to reach the Final Four. After beating University of North Carolina at Charlotte in the national semifinals, Maguire's team upset Dean Smith's (b.1931) favored North Carolina (Chapel Hill) Tar Heels, 67–59, in the title game. Warriors guard Butch Lee

scored 19 points in the final game and was named the tournament's most outstanding player, but the real star was Maguire, who openly wept as the clock ticked down to his first national championship.

Until Marquette's surge, the University of San Francisco Dons were the story of the college basketball season. Super sophomores Bill Cartwright, Winfred Boynes, and James Hardy helped carry the Dons to 29 consecutive victories and no defeats and the top spot in the polls heading into their last game of the regular season at the University of Notre Dame. But the Irish of Notre Dame rode a boisterous crowd (which was named the "player" of the game by NBC, the network that televised the contest) to an 83–72 victory that ended the Dons' hopes for an unbeaten season. Then, San Francisco's year came to a crashing halt with a 121–95 loss to University of Nevada-Las Vegas (which ended up in the Final Four) in the NCAA tournament. After starting the year 29–0, the Dons finished 29–2, losing the two games that counted most.

The Doctor Is In (the NBA, That Is)

The Portland Trail Blazers won the championship of the new-look National Basketball Association by beating the Philadelphia 76ers in six games in the finals, capped by a 109–107 victory on June 5.

As part of the merger agreement with the ABA, the NBA incorporated four teams and a host of the defunct league's stars for the 1976–77 season. The biggest of those stars was stylish forward Julius Erving (b.1950), known as "Doctor J," who had helped carry the New York Nets to the ABA title the season before. Although the Nets were one of the former ABA teams to join the NBA, Erving's contract was sold to the 76ers after a bitter contract dispute with New York.

Erving, the top scorer in the ABA's final season, continued to display his elegant game in his new league. He made a dramatic debut in his first NBA All-Star Game on February 13, earning most valuable player honors after scoring 30 points in 30 minutes. In the regular season, he averaged 21.6 points per game and led the 76ers to 50 victories and the Eastern Conference championship.

But Erving and the 76ers were upstaged in the NBA Finals by Bill Walton (b.1952) and the Trail Blazers. Portland had finished second to the Los Angeles Lakers in the Pacific Division during the regular season. In the conference finals, though, Portland brushed Los Angeles aside in four games. Then, against Philadelphia in the championship series, the Trail Blazers became the first team in NBA history to win four consecutive playoff games after losing the first two.

Walton, the finals MVP, averaged 18.6 points and a league-best 14.4 rebounds per game during the regular season. He also led the league in blocked shots.

Seattle Slew and Stevie Wonder

Jockey Jean Cruguet rode Seattle Slew to an easy four-length victory in the Belmont Stakes on June 11 to win

House Call *Philadelphia 76ers forward Julius Erving, better known as "Doctor J," drives to the basket in the NBA Finals. Erving's team was upended by Bill Walton (32) and the Portland Trail Blazers, however.*

horse racing's coveted Triple Crown. Seattle Slew became only the 10th horse in history to win all three races—the Kentucky Derby, Preakness Stakes, and Belmont Stakes—in the same year. He was the first to do so while never having lost a race.

The 1977 Horse of the Year shared racing's spotlight with jockey Steve Cauthen (b.1960). The 17-year-old sensation rode more than 400 winners to more than $6 million in earnings that year—no other rider ever had reached the $5 million

Mr. 59

Al Geiberger became the first golfer to score a 59 in a PGA event when he fired 11 birdies (one shot under par) and an eagle (two shots under par) in the second round of the Memphis Golf Classic on June 10.

Geiberger started the day with a birdie at the 10th hole (he played the second nine holes on the course first), made six birdies and an eagle in a seven-hole stretch from his sixth through 12th holes, then made an eight-foot birdie putt on the ninth hole to cap his round.

Two other players—Chip Beck and David Duval—have since equaled Geiberger's feat in PGA competition. But ever since his magical day, Geiberger is the one who has been known throughout the golfing world as "Mr. 59."

mark in a single year. Cauthen won the Eclipse Award as the nation's top jockey, earned the Associated Press male Athlete of the Year award, and was named Sports Illustrated's Sportsman of the Year.

Americans Battle Across the Pond

Tom Watson won the British Open golf tournament at Turnberry, Scotland, July 9 when he edged Jack Nicklaus (b.1940) in one of the most memorable head-to-head battles in golf history.

After both players had third-round scores of 65 to enter the final day all even, Nicklaus forged one stroke ahead after 15 holes of the fourth round. But Watson drilled a 60-foot birdie putt to pull even on hole 16, then followed with another birdie on 17 to take the lead. When Nicklaus had trouble with his drive at hole 18 and Watson put his second shot two feet from

the hole, the tournament was all but over. Still, Nicklaus made a long putt to force Watson to sink his short putt for a birdie. Watson made it to finish with a final-round 65, one stroke better than his formidable rival.

Watson also won the prestigious Masters golf tournament in 1977. Hubert Green won the United States Open, while Lanny Wadkins captured the final major of the season, the PGA Championship.

The 30-30-30-30 Club

In his final at-bat of the regular season on October 2, Los Angeles Dodgers outfielder Dusty Baker hit his 30th home run of the year off Houston Astros pitcher J.R. Richard. Baker's home run could not avert a 6–3 defeat, but it made Los Angeles the first team to have four players with 30 or more home runs in the same season.

First baseman Steve Garvey (b.1948) led the way with 33 home runs, while outfielder Reggie Smith added 32 and third baseman Ron Cey joined Baker with 30. The Dodgers won 98 games and cruised to the National League West title by 10 games. They beat the Philadelphia Phillies in four games in the League Championship Series before losing to the New York Yankees in the World Series late in October.

Soccer Explosion

International soccer star Pelé, now with the North American Soccer League's New York Cosmos, retired after the 1977 season. In his farewell match, an exhibition at Giants Stadium on October

1, he played one half for the Cosmos and one half for Santos, the Brazilian club with whom he started his career more than 20 years earlier.

Pelé's arrival in the United States two years earlier had kicked off the first true soccer boom in the country. For the first time, fans on major television networks and in large U.S. stadiums watched a good pro soccer league. The talent level was far below long-established European or South American leagues, but by bringing in top stars such as Pelé, England's George Best, and Italy's Giorgio Chinaglia, the NASL tried to bring star power to the sport.

The experiment was short-lived, but the effects continue to this day. The American Youth Soccer Organization enjoyed a huge boom in the wake of the NASL and today soccer ranks as perhaps the most popular recreational team sport among young people. In 1994, the U.S. hosted the World Cup, the quadrennial international championship, and in 2002, the national team reached the quarterfinals of the tournament, its best finish ever. The birth of Major League Soccer in 1997 harkened back to the NASL (which folded in 1982), but promised a longer life than that early pro soccer pioneer.

The Bronx Zoo

Star Wars was the year's big box-office smash, but another kind of star wars debuted in New York, where the Yankees signed high-profile free agent Reggie Jackson (b.1946) to a lucrative contract. The tempestuous Jackson combined with fiery manager Billy Martin

(1928–1989) and other high-profile personalities in the Yankees' organization to form a volatile mix that threatened to undermine the team's fortunes.

The clubhouse was dubbed "The Bronx Zoo" because of the constant bickering among Jackson, Martin, owner George Steinbrenner (b.1930), catcher Thurman Munson (1947–1979), and others. In the end, though, the team fed off the atmosphere to win its first World Series in 15 years.

New York, which had won 100 games during the regular season to edge the

Three for Three *New York Yankees slugger Reggie Jackson put on a memorable power display at the World Series when he blasted three home runs on three successive swings in the decisive sixth game.*

1977

Baltimore Orioles and the Boston Red Sox by two-and-a-half games in the American League's Eastern Division, outlasted the Kansas City Royals in a taut pennant race. The Yankees scored three runs in the ninth inning of the fifth and final game to win 5–3 and wrest the pennant from the Royals' clutches.

Jackson struggled against Kansas City's pitching in the league series, but he made the World Series against the Dodgers his personal stage, on which he batted .450 with five home runs and eight RBI. The Yankees won in six games, and Jackson's performance in the finale (see box) was one of the most memorable in World Series history.

The Yankees won the final game 8–4 to take the World Series for a record 21st time, but for the first time since 1962.

Lucky Green

A little wearing o' the green helped catapult the University of Notre Dame to college football's national title. So did future Pro Football Hall of Famer Joe Montana (b.1956), who took over at quarterback for the Irish in 1977 and passed for 1,715 yards and 12 touchdowns.

Mr. October

Reggie Jackson's reputation as a star in the postseason earned him the nickname "Mr. October," and his World Series game six dramatics while playing for the New York Yankees in 1977 was a signature performance. After drawing a walk in his first plate appearance that night against the Los Angeles Dodgers, Jackson belted a two-run home run off Los Angeles starting pitcher Burt Hooton in the fourth inning to put the Yankees ahead for good. The next inning, he slugged another two-run homer off reliever Elias Sosa. Then, in the eighth, with the Yankees' title well in hand, he punctuated the night with a solo home run off Charlie Hough. All the home runs came on the first pitch. The final scorecard: three home runs in three at bats off three consecutive pitches from three different pitchers.

It was no surprise that Jackson was such a World Series star, because he thrived in the spotlight. For his career, Jackson batted .357 with 10 home runs in 98 World Series at bats. He was the World Series MVP in 1973 (while with the Oakland A's) and 1977, set a career record for slugging percentage (.755), and played on five championship teams.

Jackson was an all-or-nothing showman who belted 563 career home runs (eighth-best all time), but also struck out an incredible 2,597 times (far and away the most in Major League history). He helped carry 10 teams to the playoffs in a 12-year span from 1971 to 1982, but he also put off teammates and fans with his bragging.

When Jackson signed a $3 million-dollar contract with the Yankees in 1977, he became baseball's highest-paid player and proclaimed himself "the straw that stirs the drink" in New York. He quickly alienated established Yankees stars with the remark. Eventually, though, he may have proved himself right.

Other Milestones of 1977

✔ Heisman Trophy-winner Tony Dorsett rushed for 202 yards and a touchdown in the University of Pittsburgh's 27–3 rout of the University of Georgia in the Sugar Bowl on New Year's Day, 1977. The Pittsburgh Panthers completed a 12–0 season and won college football's national championship for 1976.

✔ Eric Heiden won the 500-meter race en route to the all-around title at the men's world speed skating championships in the Netherlands in February. Heiden became the first American to win the crown in the 76-year history of the event. He repeated as champion in 1978 and 1979, then won five gold medals at the 1980 Winter Olympics.

✔ Sixteen-year-old American Linda Fratianne won the women's world figure skating championship in Tokyo in March.

✔ Janet Guthrie became the first woman to drive in the Indianapolis 500 on May 29. She completed only 27 laps, however, before engine trouble forced her car

Janet Guthrie

out of the race. A.J. Foyt took the checkered flag to become the first four-time winner of the famed auto race.

✔ St. Louis Cardinals outfielder Lou Brock became baseball's all-time leading base stealer when he stole two bases against the San Diego Padres on August 29. Brock surpassed Hall of Famer Ty Cobb, who held the previous record with 892 career steals.

✔ The Chicago Bears' Walter Payton rushed for 275 yards during his team's 10–7 victory over the Minnesota Vikings on November 20. Payton's prolific day established an NFL single-game record that stood for 23 years.

✔ Charlie's Angels, mood rings, and disco music were big in 1977. The year also gave us the high five. When the Los Angeles Dodgers' Dusty Baker hit his 30th home run of the season on October 2 (see page 70), he was met at home plate by fellow outfielder Glenn Burke. The two slapped palms high above their heads, and a new cultural phenomenon was born.

The Fighting Irish began the season on September 10 with a victory over defending national champion University of Pittsburgh. But they followed that with a loss at the University of Mississippi on September 17, and generally were unimpressive even though they carried a 4–1 record into midseason.

Notre Dame's fortunes surged against fifth-ranked University of Southern California (USC) on October 22, when the Irish team sprinted from their tunnel in green jerseys instead of the traditional blue. The crowd went wild—and so did the Irish. Notre Dame breezed to a 49–19 rout and was hardly challenged after that. The Irish won their last seven games by an average margin of nearly 34 points and finished 11–1. Although five other teams also finished with only one loss, Notre Dame's 38–10 rout of the previously undefeated University of Texas Longhorns in the Cotton Bowl on January 2, 1978, earned the Irish enough votes to win the national championship.

1978

College Football's Split Decision

The fifth-ranked University of Notre Dame's 38–10 rout of the top-ranked University of Texas Longhorns in the Cotton Bowl on January 2 lifted Notre Dame to a controversial national title for 1977 (see page 73). It also presaged more controversy in 1978 that fueled cries for a national playoff for college football.

This time, it was the University of Alabama Crimson Tide and the University of Southern California (USC) Trojans who were in the eye of the storm. Alabama was ranked number one early in the season, when the Trojans traveled to Tuscaloosa on September 23 and emerged with a convincing 24–14 victory. But USC, which was ranked seventh entering the game, never made it to number one because the Trojans were upset by Arizona State University three weeks later.

USC and Alabama finished the season with just the one loss, and the result was a split national championship. The Associated Press writers' poll awarded the top spot to the Crimson Tide, while United Press International's poll of coaches had the Trojans at number one.

Doomsday for Denver

The Dallas Cowboys used a relentless "Doomsday Defense" to defeat the Denver Broncos 27–10 in Super Bowl XII in New Orleans on January 15. The Super Bowl was played in New Orleans for the fourth time, but was held indoors for the first time, at the Louisiana Superdome, the home of the NFC's Saints.

The Cowboys' defense sacked Broncos quarterbacks Craig Morton and Norris Weese four times, intercepted four of Morton's passes, and recovered four fumbles. In one stretch of the second quarter, Denver turned over the ball on five consecutive possessions.

It was a reversal of fortune for the Broncos, who had used their "Orange Crush" defense to sweep to the best record in the AFC during the 1977 season.

Except for Golden Richards' brilliant fingertip grab of a touchdown pass from Staubach midway through the fourth quarter, Dallas' offense was almost an afterthought in the Super Bowl. Defensive end Harvey Martin and defensive tackle Randy White shared Super Bowl MVP honors for the Cowboys, who limited Denver to 156 total yards.

Chin Music *Leon Spinks (right) beat Muhammad Ali in February, but Ali bounced back to win the rematch.*

Ali: Down then Up

Muhammad Ali was perhaps past his prime, and some felt he should have retired. But he fought on, and on February 15 suffered perhaps the most stunning defeat of his career. Leon Spinks, an Olympic gold medalist as well-known for his gap-toothed grin as his punching power, defeated the champion in a huge upset in Las Vegas. Suddenly, Spinks was the heavyweight champion.

His sudden rise made him a media celebrity, and he appeared nearly everywhere, from TV shows to magazine covers. Throughout the summer, speculation raged as to whether Ali would come back yet again to regain his title.

On September 16, however, in a hugely hyped rematch, the two men met in New Orleans, where the 36-year-old Ali became the first man to win the heavyweight title for a third time. Though Ali would continue boxing for three more

Seventh Heaven *Washington Bullets forward Elvin Hayes grabs hold of the NBA championship trophy after his team beat the Seattle SuperSonics in seven games in the league finals.*

years, his unanimous decision over Spinks was perhaps the final culmination of perhaps the greatest and most influential career of any athlete in sports history.

Givens Goes Wild

The University of Kentucky Wildcats capped a 30–2 season with a 94–88 victory over the Duke University Blue Devils in the championship game of college basketball's NCAA tournament on March 27 in St. Louis.

Guard Jack "Goose" Givens was the star for the Wildcats in the final game. Givens poured in 23 points, many of them from long range, to help Kentucky build a seven-point halftime lead. The Wildcats never looked back. Givens finished the game with 41 points. Center Rick Robey added 20 points and 11 rebounds.

Kentucky became the fifth school in as many seasons to win the NCAA championship, since UCLA's record run of seven straight titles ended with its 1973 crown. The Wildcats had won their first national championship since 1958.

Cinderella Series

A professional basketball season that began with a black eye ended with a feel-good story when a pair of Cinderella teams, the Washington Bullets and the Seattle SuperSonics, played a thrilling, seven-game NBA Finals. The Bullets prevailed by winning the final game on June 7, 105–99.

Early in the season (on December 9, 1977), a vicious punch from the Los Angeles Lakers' Kermit Washington put the Houston Rockets' Rudy Tomjanovich in the intensive care unit of the hospital for several days.

At the same time, the SuperSonics were suffering through a miserable start that resulted in 17 losses in their first 22 games. But then former playing star Lenny Wilkens (b.1937) stepped out of the front office and onto the bench as coach. Wilkens revamped Seattle's lineup, sparking a remarkable turnaround that produced a 42–18 record the rest of the way.

Meanwhile, back East, the Bullets' veteran center Wes Unseld and electrifying forward Elvin Hayes (b.1945) took their team to the conference championship. In the finals, the SuperSonics held a three games to two lead and headed home for games six and seven. But the Bullets, who had been swept in their only two previous finals appearances, breezed to a 35-point rout to tie the series, then became just the third team in history to win a seventh game on the road.

Chris Evert: Tennis' Girl-Next-Door

The United States Open tennis tournament moved from Forest Hills to Flushing Meadows, New York, but the change in venue had little effect on Chris Evert (b.1954), the three-time defending champion. Evert closed out a record-tying fourth consecutive title with a 7–6, 6–2 victory over Wendy Turnbull on August 29. It was the first time in more than four decades that a women's tennis player won the Open four consecutive years.

Evert was America's tennis sweetheart, the girl-next-door who first wowed the crowds at the U.S. Open as a 16-year-old amateur with a quaint two-handed backhand in 1971—the year she first reached the semifinals. Her unique combination of grace and grit made her a marketing favorite, and she earned millions in endorsements off the court.

She was a huge success on the court, too, where she amassed more than $9 million in career earnings. She won 157 singles titles, including at least one Grand Slam championship (the Grand Slam is the Australian, French, and U.S. Opens, plus Wimbledon) for 13 consecutive years from 1974 to 1986.

In 1974, she forged a 54-match winning streak and was ranked number one in the world for the first time in 1975. That began her three-year run atop the rankings. But by 1978, a new challenger was on the horizon. She was Martina Navratilova (b.1956), a 21-year-old native of Czechoslovakia who had defected to the United States during the 1975 U.S. Open.

Navratilova served notice of her arrival at Wimbledon in 1978, when she came from behind to defeat Evert 2–6, 6–4, 7–5 and win her first major singles title. The Czech pushed her way to number one in the world the same year. She was number one for 331 weeks in her career, second in history only to Steffi Graf (b.1969).

Navratilova's matches with Evert highlighted women's tennis for years to come.

Scoring Spree

The race for the NBA scoring title in 1978 made for some unusual last-day drama on April 9. The Denver Nuggets' David Thompson entered the final day just a shade behind the San Antonio Spurs' George Gervin, but Denver had a day game scheduled against the Detroit Pistons, while San Antonio would not play until the evening against the New Orleans Jazz.

In the afternoon game, Thompson scored a remarkable 73 points—equaling the third-best single-game performance in league history—in a 139–137 loss. Unless Gervin could score 58 points in the nighttime game, Thompson had the title. But Gervin left little room for doubt. He had 53 points by halftime and finished with 63 points in his team's 153–132 defeat.

Gervin thus won the title by the narrowest of margins. He finished with a season scoring average of 27.22 points per game. Thompson finished at 27.15.

1978

The Triple Crown Is Affirmed

Affirmed won a thrilling battle against Alydar in the Belmont Stakes on July 10 to become the 11th horse to win thoroughbred racing's Triple Crown. The winner was ridden by jockey Steve Cauthen, the teen sensation who had burst onto the racing scene with a record-setting year in 1977 (see page 69).

Affirmed also edged Alydar in the Kentucky Derby and the Preakness Stakes (the first two legs of the Triple Crown). The Belmont turned out to be purely a two-horse match, as Affirmed and Alydar pulled away from the rest of the field and sped side-by-side down the stretch. Affirmed, racing on the inside, reached the finish line just a head before Alydar.

The Belmont winner thus became racing's second Triple Crown champion in as many years, after Seattle Slew in 1977, and its third in six years. But through 2003—despite a series of close calls—there hasn't been another Triple Crown winner.

Seattle Slew and Affirmed met in the first matchup of Triple Crown champions when they both raced in the Marlboro Cup in Belmont Park on September 16. The winner: Seattle Slew. The 1977 Horse of the Year beat the 1978 Horse of the Year by three lengths.

The Bronx Zoo, Part II

The previous season's atmosphere in the New York Yankees' clubhouse—also known as the Bronx Zoo (see page 71)—didn't change in 1978, and neither did the end result: a World Series championship for the powerful club.

Star outfielder Reggie Jackson and manager Billy Martin continued to knock heads, and the feud boiled over on July 17, when Jackson tried to bunt, against Martin's orders, and popped out. The manager suspended the player the next day.

Six days later, after Jackson returned, reporters asked Martin about Jackson and team owner George Steinbrenner. "The two deserve each other," Martin said. "One's a born liar [Martin meant Jackson] and the other's convicted [Steinbrenner got into trouble for an illegal contribution to a presidential campaign]." That remark cost Martin his job.

Match Race   *The Belmont Stakes came down to two horses in the stretch. Affirmed (on the inside) held off Alydar by a head to win horse racing's coveted Triple Crown.*

Little Man's Big Hit

Yankees shortstop Bucky Dent, who was certainly not known as a power hitter, earned himself a place in New York Yankees' lore—and the undying anger of Boston Red Sox' fans everywhere—with an unlikely home run in a playoff game between the two teams on October 2.

After the teams finished the regular season tied atop the American League East with identical records of 99–63, they met at Boston's Fenway Park for one game to determine who would advance to the League Championship Series. The Red Sox led 2–0 behind ace Mike Torrez until Dent came to the plate with two men on and two outs in the top of the seventh inning. Dent, who was batting ninth in the lineup, had hit only four home runs in the season's first 162 games. But he lofted a high fly ball to left field that disappeared into the netting above the huge wall in Fenway known as the Green Monster, for a three-run home run that stunned the Boston crowd. The Yankees did not relinquish the lead, and won the division with a 5–4 victory.

He was replaced by Bob Lemon. The Yankees, who had trailed the division-leading Boston Red Sox by as many as 14 games in mid-July, rallied to go 52–21 the rest of the way under Lemon and won the American League East.

New York ousted the Kansas City Royals in the American League Championship Series for the third consecutive year to advance to the World Series. The Yankees then overcame a two games to none deficit to the Los Angeles Dodgers by winning four straight games in October, to capture their record 22nd title.

Pitcher Ron Guidry had one of the most dominating seasons in baseball history for the Yankees. He posted a remarkable 25–3 record during the regular season, with an earned-run average of 1.74 and 248 strikeouts in 273.2 innings.

New Game in Town

The WNBA of the 1990s and 2000s was not the first women's professional basketball league in the United States. That distinction belongs to the Women's Professional Basketball League (the WBL), which tipped off on December 9 with a game between the visiting Chicago Hustle and the Milwaukee Does. A crowd of nearly 8,000 at the Milwaukee Arena watched the Does prevail, 92–87.

The WBL's inaugural season featured eight teams: Chicago Hustle, Dayton Rockettes, Houston Angels, Iowa Cornets, Milwaukee Does, Minnesota Fillies, New Jersey Gems, and New York Stars. None of the teams proved financially sound, however, and the league lasted only three seasons. The Hustle, Fillies, and Gems were the only franchises to survive all three years.

Golfers' Earnings Soar

Long before Tiger Woods burst onto the golf scene in the late 1990s, another minority golfer dominated the sport. It was Nancy Lopez, a 1978 rookie who boosted the visibility of the LPGA and became a hero to Mexican Americans.

1978

Lopez dominated her sport by winning nine tournaments—including five in a row in one stretch—and setting an earnings record with more than $189,000. She became the first LPGA player to win Rookie of the Year and Player of the Year honors in the same season.

On the men's side, Tom Watson also set a record by earning $362,000 in 1978. He won five tournaments. Watson's top rival, Jack Nicklaus, won the British Open at historic St. Andrews in Scotland in July. Nicklaus' third British Open title made him the first player to win all four of golf's major tournaments (the Masters, U.S. Open, British Open, and PGA Championship) three times.

Minority Report *Golfer Nancy Lopez became a hero to Mexican-Americans when she dominated play in a record-setting season on the women's tour.*

Pete Rose's Hit Parade

Cincinnati Reds infielder Pete Rose (b.1941) had a memorable year in 1978. On May 5, he singled off Montreal's Steve Rogers for the 3,000th hit of his big-league career. Then, on June 14, Rose had a pair of hits in the Reds' 3–1 victory over the Chicago Cubs. It would have been only a footnote for a player who entered the game hitting a modest .267—except that it began a streak in which Rose eventually hit in 44 consecutive games.

Rose's lengthy hit string equaled the longest in National League history (Wee Willie Keeler also hit in 44 straight in 1897), and was the greatest assault to date on New York Yankees great Joe DiMaggio's record 56-game streak in 1941. Rose hit .385 in his streak, which ended when he went hitless in four at-bats against the Atlanta Braves' Larry McWilliams and Gene Garber on August 1.

Rose parlayed his brilliant season into a lucrative contract. On December 5, he left the Reds, the team with whom he began his big-league career in 1963, to sign with the Philadelphia Phillies as a free agent. His four-year, $3.2 million contract was the largest in history at the time of his signing.

Rose played through 1986 and had a record 4,256 hits. But he was barred from the Baseball Hall of Fame and in 1989 was banned for life from the game by then-commissioner A. Bartlett Giamatti for allegedly gambling on baseball (allegations he long denied, but eventually admitted to in an autobiography released in January, 2004) during his tenure as a manager from 1984 to 1989.

Other Milestones of 1978

✔ The roof of the Hartford Civic Center in Connecticut collapsed from a snowstorm early in the morning hours of January 18. Luckily, no one was in the home of the World Hockey Association's Hartford Whalers. The arena had hosted a college basketball game between the University of Connecticut and the University of Massachusetts the night before.

✔ San Francisco Giants first baseman Willie McCovey hit the 500th home run of his major league career in a game against the Atlanta Braves on June 30. McCovey became only the 12th player to reach the 500 mark.

✔ Men's tennis rivals Bjorn Borg and Jimmy Connors slugged it out in singles finals at both Wimbledon and the U.S. Open. Borg won his third consecutive Wimbledon championship with a straight-set victory in July; Connors avenged the loss with a straight-set victory to win his second U.S. Open in a row in September.

✔ Nineteen-year-old John McEnroe upset Bjorn Borg, the number-one tennis player in the world, to help the United States defeat Sweden in a Davis Cup tie in October. McEnroe then helped deliver the championship with two singles victories in the finals against Great Britain in December.

✔ Long-time Ohio State Buckeyes' football coach Woody Hayes was fired after he punched an opposing player during his team's 17–15 loss to Clemson University in the Gator Bowl on December 29. Hayes had guided Ohio State to 205 victories, including two national championships, in 28 seasons.

Jimmy Connors

The Year in Wheels

American drivers in several big auto racing series came up with dramatic and historic victories during the year:

Cale Yarborough became the first driver to win three consecutive NASCAR points championships. NASCAR also began to get more national television coverage, beginning to look ahead to its dramatic rise in prominence in the 1990s.

Indy car racer Al Unser won the Indianapolis, Pocono, and Ontario 500s in 1978. No other driver had won all three in the same year. Indy-cars are "open-wheel" racers, unlike stock cars, which are modeled after passenger-car models.

Mario Andretti became the first American in 17 years to win the Grand Prix driving championship. The Grand Prix (now called Formula 1) is held at tracks around the world, and is perhaps the international "glamour king" of auto racing. Andretti remains one of the few Americans to have succeeded in the sport. His championship was tempered, however, by the death of his teammate, Ronnie Peterson, who died of complications from injuries suffered in a crash at the Italian Grand Prix on September 10. While racing continued to be glamorous and exciting, incidents like that one reminded everyone of its inherent dangers as well.

1979

Super Super Bowl

The Super Bowl was turning into a Super Dud with a series of lopsided games in recent years. But the Pittsburgh Steelers and the Dallas Cowboys put on a thrilling show at the Orange Bowl in Miami on January 21, with the Steelers winning Super Bowl XIII 35–31.

This was the first Super Bowl rematch—the teams had played in the title game three years earlier, with the Steelers winning 21–17—and one of pro football's fiercest rivalries was under way. It was fueled by pregame comments from Dallas linebacker Thomas "Hollywood" Henderson, who derisively claimed that Pittsburgh quarterback Terry Bradshaw (b.1948) "couldn't spell cat if you spotted him the c and the a."

Bradshaw had the last laugh, though, passing for Super Bowl records of 318 yards and four touchdowns to earn the game's most valuable player award (he won the award again a year later after leading the Steelers past the Rams in Super Bowl XIV).

Bradshaw completed 17 of his 30 passes against the Cowboys, including a game-tying, 75-yard strike to John Stallworth in the second quarter. Then he put the Steelers ahead 21–14—a lead they never relinquished—with a seven-yard throw to Rocky Bleier just 26 seconds before halftime.

"Go ask Thomas Henderson if I was dumb," Bradshaw told reporters after the game.

Although Pittsburgh built a 35–17 lead in the fourth quarter, the Steelers still had to survive a late rally engineered by Dallas quarterback Roger Staubach, who had mastered the art of the comeback. Staubach, who also completed 17 of 30 pass attempts for 228 yards, passed for two touchdowns in the final two and a half minutes of the game, but Pittsburgh recovered an onside kick in the closing seconds to become the first team to win the Super Bowl three times.

"The guys in the ties and dark suits [the Cowboys] against the guys in the hardhats and rolled-up sleeves [the Steelers]," was how Dallas free safety Cliff Harris described the contest. "That contrast, that was the thing between us." That "thing" was one of the NFL's classic rivalries. The Cowboys did not get their Super Bowl revenge until they beat Pittsburgh 27–17 in Super Bowl XXX in January 1996.

Super Steelers *Quarterback Terry Bradshaw (12) led the Pittsburgh Steelers past Dallas in Super Bowl XIII.*

Road Rage at the Daytona 500

The Daytona 500 on February 18 was the first NASCAR race to be televised from start to finish. Ironically, it was what happened after the race that most people remember. Race leaders Donnie Allison and Cale Yarborough battled each other in a head-to-head duel for much of the second part of the race. On the final lap, Allison had the lead but knew Yarborough would try to pass him down low on the backstretch. When Yarborough made his move, Allison was there to block his path. The two whacked together, sending Yarborough's car into the infield grass. When he tried to get back onto the track, the cars collided again.

The beneficiary of all this was Richard Petty, who was in third place.

1979

Petty sped past Allison and Yarborough to take the checkered flag.

Just then, the cameras cut to the infield, where Yarborough had gotten out of his car to confront Allison. Allison's brother, Bobby, who also was in the race, stopped by in his car. Yarborough and the two Allison brothers went at each other until they could be separated by track personnel.

"It's the worst thing I've ever seen," an incensed Yarborough told reporters afterward. "I had Donnie set up perfectly, and he knew it."

Not surprisingly, Allison had a different view, insisting that he was just trying to force Yarborough to take the high side. "When he went low, he went off the track, lost control, and hit me."

Viewers didn't care who was at fault. They were thrilled at the spectacle, and NASCAR was on its way to becoming a national sport.

Sneak Preview *When Michigan State and Indiana State met for the NCAA championship, stars Earvin "Magic" Johnson (33) and Larry Bird (dribbling) squared off for a title for the first of many times.*

Bird and Magic

Basketball guard Earvin "Magic" Johnson (b.1959) and his Michigan State Spartans met forward Larry Bird (b.1956) and his Indiana State Sycamores in the NCAA men's championship game in Salt Lake City, Utah, on March 26. Johnson and the Spartans won the game 75–64. The matchup was a hint of the epic battles between these two superstars that would continue for years to come in the NBA.

Johnson was a 6-foot-8 point guard who was versatile enough to play anywhere on the court. After he scored 24 points, grabbed seven rebounds, and handed out five assists in the final game, he was named the tournament's most outstanding player.

At 6-foot-9, Bird was more of a classic forward with a deft shooting touch and a nose for the ball. He scored 35 points in the national semifinal game as Indiana State improved to 33–0 by edging DePaul University, 76–74. In the final, though, he had to deal with constant double-teaming from Michigan State's defense. Although he led the Sycamores with 19 points and 13 rebounds, he made only seven of 21 shots.

Johnson, though only a sophomore, decided to turn pro and joined the Los Angeles Lakers for the 1979–80 season. Bird signed with the Boston Celtics, who had drafted him the previous year. Either Johnson's Lakers or Bird's Celtics won eight of the next nine NBA titles.

Batting Practice at Wrigley Field

Fantasy baseball wasn't yet a national phenomenon in 1979, but the select few participating then had to be delighted with the box score from Chicago on May 17, when the hometown Cubs outlasted the Philadelphia Phillies 23–22—delighted, of course, as long as their rosters didn't include any of the pitchers involved.

Philadelphia third baseman Mike Schmidt (b.1949) hit a solo home run in the top of the 10th inning off the Cubs' Bruce Sutter to lift the Phillies to the victory. It was the 11th home run of the game, equaling the major league record. The barrage of homers was triggered by an 18-mile-per-hour wind that was blowing out to left at Wrigley Field.

Chicago's Dave Kingman slugged three home runs, while Schmidt had two. Other notes from the box score: Shortstop Larry Bowa had five hits, catcher Bob Boone drove in five runs, and center fielder Garry Maddox had four hits in four at-bats with four RBI for the Phillies; Bill Buckner drove in seven runs and Kingman added six RBI for the Cubs. Chicago starting pitcher Dennis Lamp allowed six runs in a third of an inning. Phillies starter Randy Lerch left the game after giving up five runs in a third of an inning—but he also homered to cap Philadelphia's seven-run outburst in the top of the first.

The teams combined for 50 hits and 97 total bases. The 45 runs scored were the most in a major league game since the Cubs beat the Phillies 26–23 at Wrigley Field on August 25, 1922.

NBA Rematch

For the second consecutive year, the Washington Bullets and the Seattle SuperSonics squared off in the NBA Finals (see page 76). This time, it was the SuperSonics who emerged with their first league championship.

Seattle did not feature a big-name superstar, relying instead on a balanced scoring attack and a stingy defense to take the team to its first Pacific Division title and a team-record 52 victories during the regular season. After dispatching the Los Angeles Lakers and the Phoenix Suns in the playoffs, the SuperSonics avenged their defeat to the defending-champion Bullets.

Washington opened the finals with a 99–97 victory at home on two free throws by Larry Wright with no time left on the clock. But Seattle stormed back to win the next four games and take the title. The decisive game was a 97–93 victory at Washington on June 1.

The SuperSonics had six players who averaged double figures in scoring during

1979

the regular season, led by guard Gus Williams' 19.2 points per game. Fellow guard Dennis Johnson was an NBA All-Defensive selection, while center Jack Sikma pulled down 12.4 rebounds per game—fifth-best in the league.

A Yankee Tragedy

The New York Yankees have put together perhaps the most successful and legendary team history in sports. However, it has occasionally also been visited by tragedy. On August 2, the Yankees' catcher and team captain, Thurman Munson, only 32 years old, was killed when the private plane he was piloting crashed shortly after takeoff in Ohio. Munson had used a day off in the team's schedule to fly home to see his family.

The death of the fiery, gruff, but popular player shocked baseball and the sports world. Death did not often visit the sports world outside of auto racing and occasionally boxing. Death off the field was rare, too, and sudden death all the more shocking. For many it quickly brought to mind the fact that while sports and games are fun and can be serious business for some, they are in the greater picture very

Mr. Hockey

When Gordie Howe (b.1928) took the ice for the Hartford Whalers at the start of the NHL season in 1979, he was 51 years old. It would be his 26th, and final, NHL season. Add in the six years Howe played in the World Hockey Association (Hartford was one of the teams that was incorporated into the NHL for the 1979–80 season), and that's a total of 32 years of major league hockey.

That's a remarkable record of longevity and will likely never be broken. It puts Howe in a class with legendary athletes such as George Blanda, who played pro football until he was 48, and Satchel Paige, who pitched regularly in Major League Baseball at a reported age of 47 (some experts insist he was even older).

Howe's career deserves more than just a footnote for defying the effects of aging, though. Much more. After all, they didn't call him "Mr. Hockey" for nothing.

From the moment he stepped onto the ice as an 18-year-old for the Detroit Red Wings in 1946, it was clear that Howe had a unique talent. In his 26 NHL seasons, he was a first- or second-team All-Star 21 times. He won six scoring titles, six Hart Memorial Trophies as the league's most valuable player, and retired as the NHL's all-time leader for goals, assists, points, and games played. Moreover, he was one of the smartest and toughest players in history, and his abilities made his teammates better: He led his NHL teams to the playoffs 20 times, and helped the Red Wings win four Stanley Cup championships in the 1950s.

Howe also enjoyed a privilege afforded no other professional hockey star in history. While he was with the WHA's Houston Aeros in 1973, his sons Marty and Mark joined him to form the only two-generation line ever on the ice. The three were reunited on the Whalers in Gordie's last year.

inconsequential in comparison to life and death.

The Yankees wore black armbands for the remainder of the season, and Munson's number was retired. For years after, his locker at Yankee Stadium remained unoccupied in tribute.

Youth Is Served

The country was slowed by an oil shortage and long lines at the gas pumps in 1979, but there was no energy crisis on the men's and women's tennis tours, where an infusion of youth made headlines at the U.S. Open in Flushing Meadows, New York in September.

On the women's side, 16-year-old Tracy Austin (b.1962) became the youngest winner of the Open when she stopped Chris Evert's four-year reign as champion with a stunning 6–4, 6–3 victory. At 16 years and nine months, Austin was three months younger than "Little Mo" Connolly was when she won the Open in 1951.

"Tracy's mental toughness was scary," Evert said years later. By 1980, Austin became the top-ranked women's player in the world.

On the men's side, 20-year-old John McEnroe (b.1959) won his first Grand Slam singles title by beating Vitas Gerulaitis in straight sets, 7–5, 6–3, 6–3. McEnroe, who went on to win the U.S. Open three consecutive years and four times in a six-year span, was the youngest men's champion in more than 30 years. McEnroe would go on to win seven Grand Slam singles titles in his career and play on 12 U.S. Davis Cup teams.

Sweet Sixteen *American Tracy Austin was just 16 years old when she won the U.S. Open singles championship. She was the youngest winner of one of tennis' most coveted titles.*

We Are Family

The Pittsburgh Pirates earned a World Series title in thrilling fashion, overtaking the Baltimore Orioles by winning three consecutive games, including game seven in Baltimore on October 17. The Pirates adopted Sister Sledge's hit single, "We Are Family," as their theme song for 1979. And there was no question who was the patriarch of the family. It was veteran slugger Willie Stargell

1979

(1940–2001), better known as "Pops" to his teammates. The 39-year-old belted 32 home runs in only 126 games during the regular season, then carried his team in the postseason, when he batted .415 with five home runs, 13 RBI, and 11 extra-base hits.

Pittsburgh won 98 games during the regular season, then breezed past the Cincinnati Reds in three games in the best-of-five League Championship Series (LCS). Stargell won the first game with an 11th-inning homer, then sparked a 7–1 rout in the final game with another home run.

Baltimore, meanwhile, reached the World Series by winning a major league-best 102 games during the regular season, then outslugging the California Angels in four games in the LCS. In the World Series, the Orioles were on the verge of a title after a six-run eighth inning led to a 9–6 victory in game four for a three-games-to-one-lead.

History was not on the Pirates' side: Only three teams had rallied from a three-to-one deficit to win a seven-game World Series. But Pittsburgh won game five, 7–1, to send the Series back to Baltimore, then forced a final game when pitchers John Candelaria and Kent Tekulve combined on a seven-hit shutout in game six.

In the decisive game, Stargell's two-run home run in the sixth inning erased a 1–0 deficit and gave Pittsburgh the lead for good. The Pirates won, 4–1.

Turnaround in Tampa

The Tampa Bay Buccaneers capped an amazing transformation by beating the Kansas City Chiefs 3–0 in a torrential downpour in Tampa on December 16 to earn the Bucs their first playoff berth in the NFL team's brief history.

Nobody expects an expansion team to be very good right away, but the Buccaneers, who had joined the league in 1976, took a new team's woes to unparalleled heights—or depths. Tampa Bay went 0–14 in its first season (no other NFL team had ever lost every game it played), then followed that up with losses in its first 12 games the next year. Such futility prompted head coach John McKay's (1923–2001) famous quip, when asked after one loss about his team's execution: "I'm in favor of it."

But by 1978, the Buccaneers showed signs of life, winning five games. Then, in 1979, Tampa Bay won its first five games of the season. McKay never abandoned his goal of combining a strong running attack with a stalwart defense, and he was rewarded when Ricky Bell rushed for 1,263 yards and the defense permitted only 14.8 points per game during the 1979 regular season.

Twice as Nice

It was a banner year for the city of Pittsburgh in 1979. After the football Steelers won Super Bowl XIII in January, the baseball Pirates won the World Series in October. Only two cities have won a Super Bowl and a World Series in the same calendar year:

YEAR	CITY	TEAMS
1969	New York	Jets (football), Mets (baseball)
1979	Pittsburgh	Steelers (football), Pirates (baseball)

In the 1969-1970 season, the New York Knicks also won the team's first NBA champsionship.

Other Milestones of 1979

✔ Alabama beat number-one Penn State 14–7 in the Sugar Bowl on January 1. The Crimson Tide's upset, coupled with USC's 17–10 victory over Michigan in the Rose Bowl, resulted in a split for college football's 1978 national championship (see page 74).

✔ The National Hockey League agreed to absorb four World Hockey Association teams as part of a merger agreement between the two rival leagues on March 22. The Edmonton Oilers, Hartford Whalers, Quebec Nordiques, and Winnipeg Jets joined the NHL for the 1979–80 season.

✔ Fuzzy Zoeller won the Masters golf tournament on April 15 in a playoff with Ed Sneed and Tom Watson. Zoeller overcame a six-stroke deficit to Sneed over the final 13 holes of regulation play, then needed two extra holes to become the first golfer to win in his first trip to Augusta since Gene Sarazen did it in 1935.

✔ The Montreal Canadiens won their fourth consecutive NHL title (and their sixth of the decade) when they beat the New York Rangers in the Stanley Cup Finals in May. The Boston Bruins (1970 and 1972) and the Philadelphia Flyers (1974 and 1975) were the only American teams to capture the Cup in the 1970s.

Fuzzy Zoeller

✔ The Houston Angels defeated the Iowa Cornets in the deciding game of the WBL Championship Series on May 1 to win the first women's pro basketball title.

✔ The Alabama Crimson Tide opened its college football schedule with a 30–6 rout of Georgia Tech in Atlanta on September 6. The Crimson Tide rolled on to 12 consecutive victories, outscoring its opponents 383–67, and leaving little room for doubt about the national champion for 1979.

✔ Former Olympic boxing champion Sugar Ray Leonard won the world welterweight title when he defeated Wilfred Benitez in Las Vegas on November 30. Leonard recorded a technical knockout when the fight was stopped six seconds before the end, and he was ahead on all the judges' scorecards as well.

A late-season three-game losing streak threatened to spoil Tampa Bay's fine start, but the Buccaneers edged the Chicago Bears for the NFC Central Division title by beating the Chiefs in the season finale. Bell rushed for 137 yards and Neil O'Donoghue kicked a 19-yard field goal to provide the only points against Kansas City.

Tampa Bay eventually reached the 1979 NFC title game. The Buccaneers fell just one victory short of qualifying for Super Bowl XIV in January 1980.

RESOURCES

1970s Events and Personalities

Champions, Cheaters, and Childhood Dreams: Memories of the All-American Soap Box Derby
By Melanie Payne (Akron, Ohio: University of Akron Press, 2003)
The author went straight to the participants for their memories of the great race.

Billie Jean King : Tennis Trailblazer
By Joanne Lannin (Minneapolis, Minnesota: Lerner Publications Company, 1999).
Billie Jean King is perhaps most widely remembered for beating Bobby Riggs in the "Battle of the Sexes" in 1973. But her far-ranging accomplishments made her a pioneer for all women athletes, not just those on the tennis court.

Watergate: Scandal in the White House (Twentieth Century American History Series)
By Barbara Silberdick Feinberg (Danbury, Connecticut: Franklin Watts, 1990)
This is a detailed look at one of the landmark events of the 1970s, or any other decade: the Watergate break-in and the resulting political scandal that eventually led to the resignation of President Richard M. Nixon

Wooden
By John R. Wooden, with Steve Jamison (New York: McGraw-Hill/ Contemporary Books, 1997).
John Wooden's basketball dynasty at UCLA peaked in the 1970s. In this book, the legendary coach offers insights into his philosophy on and off the court.

American Sports History

The Complete Book of the Olympics
By David Wallechinsky (New York: Viking Penguin, 2000)
An extremely detailed look at every Winter and Summer Olympics from 1896 to the present, including complete lists of medal winners and short biographies of important American and international athletes.

The Encyclopedia of North American Sports History
Edited by Ralph Hickok (New York: Facts On File, 1992)
This title includes articles on the origins of all the major sports as well as capsule biographies of key figures.

Encyclopedia of Women and Sport in America
Edited by Carol Oglesby et al. (Phoenix: Oryx Press, 1998)
A large overview of not only key female personalities on and off the playing field, but a look at issues surrounding women and sports.

Encyclopedia of World Sport
Edited by David Levinson and Karen Christensen (New York: Oxford University Press, 1999)
This wide-ranging book contains short articles on an enormous variety of sports, personalities, events, and issues, most of which have some connection to American sports history. This is a great starting point for additional research.

Facts and Dates of American Sports

By Gordon Carruth and Eugene Ehrlich (New York: Harper & Row, 1988)
Very detailed look at sports history, focusing on when events occurred. Large list of birth and death dates for major figures.

The Sporting News Chronicle of 20th Century Sports

By Ron Smith (New York: BDD/Mallard Press, 1992)
A good single-volume history of key sports events. They are presented as if written right after the event, thus giving the text a "you are there" feel.

Sports of the Times

By David Fischer and William Taafe. (New York: Times Books, 2003)
A unique format tracks the top sports events on each day of the calendar year. Find out the biggest event for every day from January 1 to December 31.

Total Baseball

Edited by John Thorn, Pete Palmer, and Michael Gershman. (New York: Total Sports, 2004, eighth edition)
The indispensable bible of baseball, it contains the career records of every Major Leaguer. Essays in the front of the book cover baseball history, team history, overviews of baseball in other countries, and articles about the role of women and minorities in the game.

Total Football

Edited by Bob Carroll, John Thorn, Craig Neft, and Michael Gershman (New York: HarperCollins, 2000)
The complete and official record of every player who has played in the NFL. The huge book also contains essays on a wide variety of topics relating to pro football.

Sports History Web Sites

ESPN.com

www.sports.espn.go.com
The Web site run by the national cable sports channel contains numerous history sections within each sport. This one for baseball is the largest and includes constantly updated statistics on baseball.

Hickok Sports

www.hickoksports.com
Not the most beautiful site and devoid of pictures, but filled with a wealth of information on sports at all levels. It is run by Ralph Hickok, an experienced sportswriter, and is regularly updated with the latest winners.

Official League Web Sites

www.nfl.com
www.nba.com
www.mlb.com
www.nhl.com
Each of the major sports leagues has history sections on their official Web sites

Official Olympics Web Site

http://www.olympic.org/uk/games/index_uk.asp
Complete history of the Olympic Games, presented by the International Olympic Committee.

The Sporting News "Vault"

www.sportingnews.com/archives
More than 100 years old, The St. Louis-based Sporting News *is the nation's oldest sports weekly. In the history section of its Web site, it has gathered hundreds of articles on sports events, championships, stars, and more. It also includes audio clips of interviews with top names in sports from yesterday and today.*

INDEX

New York Mets, 88
New York Nets, 62, 69
New York Rangers, 89
New York Renaissance, 32
New York Stars, 79
New York Yankees, 36–38, 47, 52,
    63, 64–65, 72, 78–79
Nicklaus, Jack, 57, 70, 80
North American Soccer League
    (NASL), 57, 70
North Carolina State, 43–44
North Sea, 41
Northwest League, 45

Oakland Athletes (A's), 47, 53–54
Oakland Raiders, 42, 48, 49, 66
O'Donoghue, Neil, 89
Ohio State, 50, 56, 58, 81
Olajuwon, Hakeem, 31
Olympics. *See* Summer Olympic
    Games; Winter Olympic
    Games
Ontario 500, 81
Or, Bobby, 12–13

Paige, Satchel, 22, 86
Palmer, Tyler, 22
Parent, Bernie, 49
Payton, Walter, 73
Pearson, David, 60, 61
Pearson, Drew, 57
Pelé, 57, 70–71
Pennsylvania State, 65, 89
Pepe, Maria, 45
Perez, Tony, 55
Peterson, Ronnie, 81
Petty, Lee, 60
Petty, Richard "The King," 44, 60,
    61, 83–84
Philadelphia Flyers
    Stanley Cups, 49, 57, 58–59, 89
Philadelphia Freedom, 11
Philadelphia Phillies, 10, 65, 85
Philadelphia 76ers, 47, 68–69
Phoenix Suns, 62, 85
Piazza, Mike, 64
ping-pong, 18–20
Pittsburgh Pirates (baseball),
    14, 22, 66–67, 87–88
Pittsburgh Pirates (football), 50
Pittsburgh Steelers, 33, 42, 49,
    50–51, 59–60, 66, 82–83, 88
Pocono 500, 81
Podolak, Ed, 22, 23
Portland Mavericks, 45–46
Portland Trail Blazers, 68, 69

Preakness Stakes, 38, 78. *See
    also* Triple Crown (horse rac-
    ing)
Prefontaine, Steve, 41, 57
Professional Golfers Association
    (PGA), 68, 70, 80
Pro Football Hall of Fame, 15,
    21, 22, 32, 40, 48, 49, 65

Quebec Nordiques, 18, 89
Queens College, 52

race relations
    black coaches of NBA title
        teams, 53
    civil rights movement, 45
    first black celebrity in nation-
        al ads, 39
    first black elected by CNBL to
        Hall of Fame, 22
    first black in Basketball Hall
        of Fame, 32
    first black MLB manager, 52,
        53
    first black professional bas-
        ketball team, 32
    Mexican-Americans in pro-
        fessional golf, 79–80
Reed, Willis, 36
Richard, J. R., 70
Richards, Golden, 74
Riggs, Bobby, 11, 41
Riordan, Mike, 53
Robey, Rick, 76
Robinson, Frank, 52, 53
rodeo, 14
Rogers, Steve, 80
Rojas, Cookie, 10
Rooney, Art "Chief," 50, 51
Rose, Pete, 80
Rose Bowl championship, 50, 58,
    89
Rosewall, Ken, 46
Rozelle, Pete, 13–15, 50, 51
Rudi, Joe, 47
Ruth, Babe, 22, 44, 45, 55
Ryan, Nolan, 37, 38, 57

Sabonis, Arvydas, 31
St. Louis Blues, 12
St. Louis Cardinals, 10
San Antonio Spurs, 62, 77
San Diego Chargers, 41
San Diego Padres, 73
San Francisco 49ers, 42
San Francisco Giants, 81

Santos, 71
Sarazen, Gene, 89
Schmidt, Mike, 65, 85
Schranz, Karl, 24
Schweitzer, Hoyle, 38
Sciarra, John, 58
Seattle Slew, 69, 78
Seattle SuperSonics, 76–77, 85–86
Secretariat, 35, 38–39
Shula, Don, 31–32, 33, 48
Sikma, Jack, 86
Simionescu, Mariana, 46
Simpson, O. J. "The Juice," 39–40
Sittler, Darryl, 65
skiing, 22, 24
Smith, Dean, 68
Smith, Reggie, 70
Smith, Robyn, 41
Smith-Court, Margaret, 11, 14
Sneed, Ed, 89
soccer, 57, 70–71
Sosa, Elias, 72
speed skating, 24, 61, 73
Spinks, Leon, 63, 75–76
Spinks, Michael, 63
Spitz, Mark, 28–29, 30
sports marketing, 22, 41, 49, 63
Stabler, Ken, 48
Stalworth, John, 82
Stanfill, Bill, 32
Stanley Cup, 86, 89
Stargell, Willie "Pops," 87–88
Staubach, Roger, 56, 57, 74, 82
Stead, Karen, 23
Steinbrenner, George, 71, 78
Stenerud, Jan, 22
Sugar Bowl, 73, 89
Sullivan Award, 36
Summer Olympic Games
    1968, 28–29
    1972, 7, 13, 28, 29–31
    1976, 59, 63
    televised games, 13
Super Bowl
    1960s, 8, 42, 88
    1970, 8
    1972, 31
    1973, 33
    1974, 42
    1975, 42, 50–51
    1976, 42, 59–60
    1977, 66
    1978, 74
    1979, 42, 82–83, 88
    1980s, 42, 82
    1990s, 42, 82